THE EDUCATION WEEK GUIDE TO

K–12 Terminology

Edited by

Mary-Ellen Phelps Deily

JOSSEY-BASS
A Wiley Imprint
www.josseybass.com

Published by Jossey-Bass

A Wiley Imprint

989 Market Street, San Francisco, CA 94103-1741—www.josseybass.com

Jossey-Bass books and products are available through most bookstores. To contact
Jossey-Bass directly call our Customer Care Department within the U.S. at 800-956-
7739, outside the U.S. at 317-572-3986, or fax 317-572-4002.

Jossey-Bass also publishes its books in a variety of electronic formats. Some content that
appears in print may not be available in electronic books.

Credits appear on page 134

Library of Congress Cataloging-in-Publication Data

The Education week guide to K-12 terminology / edited by Mary-Ellen
Phelps Deily. – 1st ed.
        p. cm.
  ISBN 978-0-470-40668-7 (alk. paper)
  1. Education–Terminology. 2. Education–Dictionaries. I. Phelps Deily, Mary-Ellen.
II. Education week.
  LB15.E335 2009
  370.3–dc22

                                                                    2008043492

Printed in the United States of America

FIRST EDITION

PB Printing   10 9 8 7 6 5 4 3 2 1

Contents

Organizations and Other Terms

Acknowledgments

Creating this guide involved pulling together a great deal of research from numerous sources. It would not have been possible without the assistance of the reporters and editors at *Education Week* and teachermagazine.org. In particular, I'd like to thank Gregory Chronister, Ann Bradley, David J. Hoff, Christina A. Samuels, Bess Keller, Vaishali Honawar, Debra Viadero, Mary Ann Zehr, Karen Diegmueller, Andrew Trotter, Mark Walsh, Naomi Cohen, Elizabeth Rich, and Stephen Sawchuk.

Preface

Welcome to the first in a new series of *Education Week* guides to critical issues in elementary and secondary learning. *Education Week* and Jossey-Bass have launched this series with what we see as the essential starting point: K–12 terminology. Before we write in depth about any one topic, we believe it's crucial that our readers understand the unique vocabulary of learning—a vocabulary that can be more complicated, nuanced, and technical than one might expect.

Education is a topic that affects and interests many. Yet communicating about it isn't always easy. Sometimes, in fact, it's downright difficult. The language of special education, for instance, is complicated, legalistic, and detailed. Testing and standards carry their own linguistic baggage, and the rising field of school technology brings with it the combined quirks of the learning and electronic worlds. In short, there's a lot of ground to cover and a lot of unusual words—and acronyms—to navigate. While no one book could cover all of the terms used in education, we've done our best to focus on the most commonly used and misunderstood language.

This book is a broad scan of the key terms that practitioners, policymakers, and parents should know. In some cases, we've coupled our definitions with excerpts from *Education Week* articles to throw more light on the terms in question. And, in the back of this guide, we've included lists of key K–12 education organizations and terms and the frequently confusing acronyms used to represent them. The alphabet soup of education is a common stumbling block for outsiders and insiders alike—we hope our lists help you make more sense of these crucial ABCs. Most important, we hope this and our upcoming guides ease and enrich your journey through K–12 learning.

Mary-Ellen Phelps Deily

Editorial Director, Education Week Press

November 2008

The Education Week

Guide to

K–12
Terminology

EDUCATION WEEK

Education Week is the nation's premier independent news source for K–12 education. Commonly referred to as "American Education's Newspaper of Record," the nonprofit newspaper has kept educators and policymakers abreast of important developments in schools for more than 27 years. *Education Week* boasts a staff of more than 30 reporters and editors, each and every one an expert in the complicated world of covering education. Increasingly, *Education Week* is focusing on coverage that seeks to help policymakers and practitioners identify "what works," promising strategies, and model programs.

Education Week Press is one arm of Editorial Projects in Education (EPE), an independent, nonprofit corporation dedicated to elevating the level of discourse on American K–12 education and best known as the publisher of *Education Week*. EPE is also the home of teachermagazine.org, TopSchoolJobs.org, Digital Directions, and the EPE Research Center, which produces the highly acclaimed *Quality Counts, Technology Counts,* and *Diplomas Counts* reports. EPE's Web site, edweek.org, is an award-winning source of up-to-the-minute news, information, and resources for educators, as well as in-depth research on issues preK–12.

A Nation at Risk

The landmark—and still controversial—report that declared a "rising tide of mediocrity" in U.S. education posed a threat to America's prosperity and status in the world.

A Nation at Risk was released April 26, 1983, by the National Commission on Excellence in Education, a body convened by the U.S. Department of Education under President Reagan's first secretary of education, Terrel H. Bell.

The strongly worded report touched a nerve with a public weary of a lingering economic crisis and deeply worried by foreign competitors. It cited Japanese efficiency in auto making, a South Korean breakthrough in steel making, and the displacement of American machine tools by German products as signs of "a redistribution of trained capability throughout the globe."

The report fueled an already-emerging campaign for improving schools as a step to a brighter future for the United States.

Abecedarian Study

A rigorous scientific study of pre-K programs in North Carolina, the Abecedarian Study revealed students who attended high-quality early education programs experienced greater academic success and educational attainment. Fifty-seven infants were randomly assigned to receive early interventions, and their outcomes were compared with a control group of fifty-four infants who did not receive such interventions. The children in the treatment group attended high-quality pre-K programs from infancy through age five.

Follow-up assessments at ages twelve and fifteen revealed that children from the treatment group had significantly higher scores in reading and mathematics, compared with the control group. Follow-up assessments with study participants at age twenty-one revealed that the students from the treatment group were more likely to have recently graduated from or be enrolled in college.

ability grouping

A common instructional practice of clustering students according to their academic skills. Ability grouping allows a teacher to provide the same level of instruction to the entire group, but debate over the fairness and effectiveness of ability grouping, also known as tracking, can be intense. The terms have been used to describe a wide array of practices, ranging from the segregation of black children at an early age, based on unfairly administered intelligence tests, to the placement of gifted and talented children from various backgrounds in advanced courses designed to challenge them.

Opponents of grouping by ability tend to use both terms pejoratively and interchangeably. But advocates for the gifted and talented and other supporters of homogeneous grouping say they, too, oppose "tracking"—by which they mean placing children at a certain academic level in most subjects at an early age and denying them an opportunity to move to a higher level. By comparison, they say, "ability grouping" is nothing more than the placement of children at certain tables or in certain classrooms where they will receive an appropriate level of instruction with classmates of similar ability. Such placements may vary from grade to grade and subject to subject. (See *tracking.*)

abstinence-only education

Education programs that focus exclusively on teaching children to abstain from sexual activity until marriage. Critics charge that failing to provide students with information about contraception is a dangerous lapse, but proponents say that comprehensive sex education encourages earlier sexual activity.

acceleration

The practice of moving students through the traditional curriculum at rates faster than the typical pace, sometimes used with students deemed "gifted."

accelerated-learning options
Programs that permit students to earn college credit while still in high school.

Accelerated Schools Project
Developed in 1986 by Henry M. Levin, then an education and economics professor at Stanford University, the program is known best for its focus on providing accelerated instruction to all children, including those labeled "at risk." The national program is now based in Storrs, Connecticut, and has satellite training centers throughout the country.

accommodations
Special provisions made for children with disabilities. A child with learning disabilities may require certain testing accommodations (such as more time to take a test or read-aloud exams) based on an individualized education program (IEP). (See *Individuals with Disabilities Education Act.*)

accountability
State or district policies related to holding districts, schools, teachers, or students responsible for performance. School and district accountability systems typically include efforts to assess and rate schools or districts based on student performance and other indicators, to publicly report on school or district performance, and to provide rewards and sanctions for schools or districts based on performance or improvement over time. Student accountability generally refers to efforts to hold students responsible for their own performance by requiring students to pass a test to be promoted from grade to grade or to graduate from high school. Teacher accountability provisions may include evaluating teachers on the basis of their students' test scores. While many agree that accountability is a noble goal, there is widespread debate over the wisdom of certain accountability measures and the pressures and consequences they impose on students, teachers, and school systems.

accreditation
Accreditation is a broad term that refers to two separate processes in education—one involving schools and school districts and the other involving schools of education.

School accreditation, which predates and is separate from the system of performance targets and sanctions set up under the federal No Child

Left Behind Act, is a process that involves meeting a set of guidelines focused on school improvement and governance that are evaluated by outside professionals, not government officials. In addition to national and regional accrediting groups, some states still accredit schools on their own, although that process has largely become part of their accountability systems for education.

By contrast, a separate process exists by which an organization, usually the National Council for the Accreditation of Teacher Education, sanctions teacher-education programs. The council had given more than 630 such programs its seal of approval for quality as of May 2008. States also approve teacher-education programs by means of issuing teaching licenses to their graduates.

Achieve

A Washington-based organization led by governors and business leaders that promotes higher academic standards. Achieve is heavily involved in work on international standards benchmarking and is studying academic expectations in other countries. (See *American Diploma Project.*)

achievement gap

The troubling performance gaps between many African American and Hispanic students, at the lower end of the performance scale, and their Asian and non-Hispanic white peers at the upper end, and the similar academic disparity between students from low-income and well-off families. The achievement gap shows up in grades, standardized-test scores, course selection, dropout rates, and college-completion rates. It has become a focal point of education reform efforts.

ACT

The ACT exam is one of the nation's two major college-entrance exams, along with the SAT. The ACT is a standardized test designed to gauge students' knowledge of high school content; it includes an optional essay. Here is a sample question:

Which of the following is equivalent to $(x)(x)(x)(x)$, for all x ?

A. $4x$

B. x^4

C. $x + 4$

D. 4^x

E. $2x^2$

© 2008, ACT Inc. The correct answer is "B."

ACT, Inc.

ACT, Inc. is the nonprofit testing organization that produces the ACT college-entrance exam, founded in 1959 as the American College Testing program. ACT, Inc. has conducted a series of studies looking at students' preparedness for college, based on the relationship between their scores on the ACT subtests, the courses the students have taken in high school, and their grades in college-level courses. In "Crisis at the Core: Preparing All Students for College and Work," released in 2004, the organization found that a majority of students who took the exam were far from ready for the academic rigors of college.

adaptive learning systems

Technology designed to reflect and respond to the learning styles of individual students. Instead of a one-size-fits-all package, these types of systems are intended to work with the needs of individual learners. (See *assistive technology*.)

adequate yearly progress

Adequate yearly progress (AYP) is the measure by which schools, districts, and states are held accountable for student performance under Title I of the No Child Left Behind Act of 2001. AYP requires states to use a single accountability system for all public schools to determine whether students on average, as well as subgroups of students, are making progress toward meeting state academic content standards, with the goal of all students being proficient in reading and mathematics by 2014. (See *No Child Left Behind Act*.)

Adult Literacy Study

A test of real-world reading and quantitative literacy that is taken by sixteen- to sixty-five-year-olds around the globe.

Advanced Placement (AP)

A series of courses administered by the College Board that high school students can take to earn college credit. Students must master a generally higher level of coursework and pass an accompanying test to earn AP credits.

affirmative action

Refers broadly to policies that are focused on race, ethnicity, and gender. Examples include making an effort to hire minorities or setting aside a percentage of public contracts for minority firms. The term was first used in the 1960s, when President Johnson and President Nixon signed executive orders requiring businesses with federal contracts to establish goals and timetables for hiring minorities. Affirmative action has also been a flashpoint in college admissions because for years colleges and universities gave preferences to certain students based on their racial or ethnic background. In 2003, the U.S. Supreme Court upheld the individual consideration of race as a factor in higher education admissions, but rejected the use of numerical point systems to promote racial and ethnic diversity. Lower federal courts and even state courts have issued conflicting rulings about the constitutionality of race-conscious policies in K–12 education in recent years. (See *desegregation.*)

alphabetics

Reading skills tied to decoding and word recognition. Alphabetics skills include phonemic awareness—recognizing that sounds in spoken language fit together to make words—and letter identification.

alternative assessment

Any form of measuring what students know and are able to do other than traditional standardized tests. Alternative forms of assessment include portfolios and performance-based assessments. (See *portfolio.*)

alternative credentials

Often called "modified diplomas" or "certificates of completion." Many states today offer alternative credentials for students with disabilities or others who do not pass high school exit exams.

alternative preparation programs

See *alternative teacher certification.*

alternative schools

This term broadly refers to public schools that are set up by states or school districts to serve populations of students who are not succeeding in the traditional public school environment. Alternative schools offer students who are failing academically or may have learning disabilities or behavioral problems an opportunity to achieve in a different setting. While there are many different kinds of alternative schools, they are often characterized by their flexible schedules, low teacher-student ratios, and modified curricula.

alternative settings

Alternative educational placements for students with disabilities who cannot receive an adequate education in the public schools. School districts must pay for alternative placement if they cannot provide the accommodations required in a student's individualized education program. (See *Individuals with Disabilities Education Act.*)

alternative teacher certification

Programs that certify teaching candidates who have not attended education schools, the traditional route for teacher preparation. The number of alternative programs that certify teachers skyrocketed from 12 in 1983 to 485 in 2006. Critics of alternative routes to teacher licensure describe them as shortcuts to teaching, fault them as lacking rigor, and say they do not provide enough clinical experience before putting teachers in classrooms. Proponents counter that such programs draw new and talented individuals to teaching.

America COMPETES Act

A federal law that seeks to bolster mathematics and science education through improved teacher recruitment and training and the promotion of successful classroom practices through federal grants for schools. America COMPETES is short for America Creating Opportunities to Meaningfully Promote Excellence in Technology, Education, and Science Act. The measure supports the Robert Noyce Scholarship Program, which provides grants of $10,000 a year to college majors in math- and science-related subjects who agree to teach in high-need schools, by expanding recipients' years of eligibility for aid and giving them more time to finish teacher training. (See *(Robert) Noyce Teacher Scholarships.*)

American Diploma Project

A multistate effort to identify the knowledge and skills high school graduates need for success in college and the workforce. The project is run by Achieve, a Washington-based organization led by governors and business leaders that promotes higher academic standards.

American Federation of Teachers (AFT)

The second-largest teachers' union in the United States, with more than 1.3 million members—not all of them teachers, however. Of the AFT's members, 200,000 work in New York City and another 350,000 work elsewhere in New York state.

American Sign Language (ASL)

A complex language of hand motions and other movements used by people with hearing impairments. ASL is the first language of many deaf North Americans.

Americans with Disabilities Act (ADA)

Signed into law in 1990 by President George H.W. Bush, the ADA is a civil rights law mandating rights and protections for people with disabilities. Title II of the law covers state and local governmental entities, including schools. The law states that entities must make reasonable accommodations to enable people with disabilities to access their services.

AmeriCorps

A national service organization. Organizations may apply for AmeriCorps support to serve critical education needs, among other priorities.

annual measurable objective (AMO)

Achievement targets set by states based on students' scores on state assessments in reading and mathematics. States set AMOs to gauge their progress toward meeting the No Child Left Behind Act's goal of "adequate yearly progress." (See *adequate yearly progress* and *No Child Left Behind Act*.)

Arts Education Partnership

A Washington, D.C.-based group of one hundred education and arts organizations, foundations, businesses, and government agencies that works to ensure a place for the arts in state school reform efforts.

assessment

An exercise—such as a written test, portfolio, or experiment—that seeks to measure a student's skills or knowledge in a subject area. Assessments are a focal point of the standards and accountability movement.

assistive technology

Technology for people with disabilities. Assistive-technology devices include a range of aids, such as wheelchairs, communication devices, and computer hardware. The federal Assistive Technology Act of 2004, overseen by the U.S. Department of Education, aims to provide more direct aid to individuals with disabilities. It also encourages states to invest in programs that have been shown to be most effective in providing assistive technology. (See *adaptive learning systems.*)

Asperger's syndrome

A disorder that falls on the autism spectrum. Students with Asperger's syndrome tend to excel in subjects that interest them, compiling amazing knowledge bases in their areas of obsession. But they require drilling in such day-to-day basics as how to make eye contact, or how to stand the appropriate distance from another child in line. The exact cause of both autism and Asperger's syndrome is unknown.

at risk

Describes students with socioeconomic challenges, such as poverty, that may place them at a disadvantage in achieving academic, social, or career goals. Such students are deemed at risk of failing, dropping out, or "falling through the cracks" at school.

ATLAS

Short for Authentic Teaching Learning and Assessment for All Students, ATLAS is a program for comprehensive, systemwide reform in schools. ATLAS focuses on five areas: teaching and learning, assessment, professional development, management and decision making, and family and community. Launched in 1992, ATLAS Communities is the brainchild of Yale University psychologist James P. Comer; Howard Gardner, a Harvard University psychology professor; Theodore R. Sizer, a Brown University professor emeritus; and Janet Whitla, a former president and chief executive officer of the Education Development Center, a research group based in Newton, Massachusetts.

attention deficit disorder (ADD)

The historical name for the disorder now known as AD/HD, which is characterized by the inability to concentrate and, in some cases, impulsiveness and hyperactivity. (The American Psychiatric Association changed the designation in 1994 to reflect new research.) Between 3 percent and 10 percent of the nation's school-age children are thought to have the disorder. The National Resource Center on AD/HD says that children labeled today as having ADD typically fall in the category of AD/HD-1, predominantly inattentive type. (See *attention deficit/ hyperactivity disorder.*)

attention deficit/hyperactivity disorder (AD/HD)

Attention deficit/hyperactivity disorder (AD/HD) is a common neuro-biological condition affecting 5–8 percent of school-age children with symptoms persisting into adulthood in as many as 60 percent of cases (that is, approximately 4 percent of adults). It is characterized by developmentally inappropriate levels of inattention, impulsivity, and hyperactivity, according to the National Resource Center on AD/HD. There are diagnostic categories within AD/HD: AD/HD predominantly inattentive type (AD/HD-I); AD/HD predominantly hyperactive-impulsive type: (AD/HD-HI); and AD/HD combined type: (AD/HD-C).

auditory processing disorder

A disorder in which an individual cannot process words or sounds (or both) in the traditional way. Previously known as CAPD—central auditory processing disorder.

autism

A complex neurological disorder that typically appears during the first three years of life. Children and adults with autism typically have difficulties in verbal and nonverbal communication, social interactions, and leisure or play activities. The disorder makes it difficult to communicate with others and to relate to the outside world. In 2007, the U.S. Centers for Disease Control and Prevention reported that nearly 6 of every 1,000 children in a federal study had an autism-spectrum disorder. The findings translated to 1 in every 150 children in the communities the CDC studied having disorders such as autism, pervasive developmental disorder (not otherwise specified), or Asperger's syndrome. The study did not provide a national estimate for the prevalence of the disorders. Previous estimates had indicated that between 1 in 500 children and 1 in 166 have an autism-spectrum disorder, federal health officials said. Studies of people with autism have shown they have abnormalities in several regions of the brain.

B

balanced reading instruction

A teaching approach incorporating a variety of skills- and literature-based reading methods. The field of reading instruction has been marked for decades by disputes over the best way to teach reading—generally speaking, a phonics-based versus literature-based approach. Over the past decade, a consensus has emerged that a balanced combination of approaches is best, although there is still considerable debate over how much skills instruction is needed.

basal readers

Elementary school books that incorporate simple stories and practice exercises to progressively reinforce what students are learning.

basic skills

The traditional building blocks of a curriculum that are most commonly associated with explicit instruction in early elementary language arts and mathematics. Basic skills have historically been taught in isolation. Basic skills include teaching the letters of the alphabet, how to sound out words, spelling, grammar, counting, adding, subtracting, and multiplying.

The Bell Curve

Hotly debated book by Richard J. Herrnstein and Charles Murray that posited that America is becoming divided into a nation of cognitive "haves" and "have nots." The book—published in 1994—ignited controversy by suggesting that blacks as a group are less intelligent than whites as it emphasized the role of heredity and race in intelligence.

benchmarking

The practice of measuring performance against a set standard; generally, in education, comparisons are based on standardized test scores. Benchmarks can help identify best practices that set the performance of one school ahead of another lower-performing school with a similar student body. In recent years, international benchmarking has become prominent as advocates seek comparisons of the achievement of American children with their peers in other countries and use those results—which often find Americans behind their peers in other developed nations—to press for change in U.S. schools.

bilingual education

An education program for children whose native language is not English. Children are taught for some portion of the day in their native language, with the goal of moving them into mainstream English classes as quickly as possible—usually within two or three years. Ideally, such programs allow students to keep up academically because they can learn subject matter in their native language while they learn English. (See *English-language learners* and *limited English proficient students.*)

Blaine amendments

Clauses in many state constitutions that restrict the flow of public money to religious schools. So-called Blaine amendments—which opponents say were motivated at least in part by anti-Catholic bias—are named for the nineteenth-century Republican political leader James G. Blaine, who strongly advocated such provisions.

block scheduling

Block scheduling increases the length of the traditional class period; it carves out more time for instruction by reducing the amount of time students spend getting from one class to another as well as the amount of time teachers spend on taking attendance and other administrative matters. Block schedules can follow a variety of patterns, including 4x4 (students take four ninety-minute classes a day and complete them in a semester rather than a full year), A/B (each semester students take eight ninety-minute classes, but classes meet every other day, four on day A and four on day B), and 75–15, 75–15 (students take four classes for a seventy-five-day fall term, followed by a fifteen-day intersession for enrichment activities or remedial work, and the pattern repeats in the spring).

blog

Short for "Web log," a blog is a publicly accessible Web page, often authored by one individual. Originally used by individuals as a form of online diary, blogs today are being used by some educators as a means of communicating with their colleagues, parents, and students. (See *multimedia* and *World Wide Web*.)

Bloom's Taxonomy

A model for classifying thinking. Benjamin S. Bloom led a group of educators tasked with developing a means of classifying thinking. The group broke thinking into three broad categories: *cognitive,* the knowledge-based domain; *affective,* the attitudinal-based domain; and *psychomotor,* the skills-based domain. Focusing on the cognitive domain, Bloom's group identified six levels of complexity in thinking. Teachers have sometimes been encouraged—based on Bloom's Taxonomy—to guide their students to higher levels of thinking and learning. First issued in 1956, the taxonomy was updated in the 1990s. (See *higher-order thinking skills*.)

Blue Ribbon Schools

Schools recognized by the U.S. Department of Education for academic excellence. Launched by the U.S. Department of Education in 1983, the Blue Ribbon Schools program has evolved from a simple recognition effort into a detailed self-analysis that some say is a valuable tool to help schools improve.

'Book Study' Helps Teachers Hone Skills

By Bess Keller
Education Week: *May 21, 2008*

At Palo Alto High School in California, about a dozen teachers talked in 2007 about Beverly Daniel Tatum's *Why Are All the Black Kids Talking Together in the Cafeteria?* In 2008, a group tackled *Mindset,* which argues against the reality of fixed intelligence and for the value of effort.

The book "is informing our teaching in how we give feedback to students: praise for effort, leading to increased growth, rather than praising on what might seem to be innate qualities," wrote Elizabeth Brimhall in an e-mail. She organized the groups as part of her school's teacher-directed staff development.

book study

A means of teacher professional development that involves teachers gathering regularly to discuss a book or books relevant to their work.

Broad Prize for Urban Education

The Broad Prize for Urban Education recognizes urban school districts that demonstrate the greatest overall performance and improvement in student achievement while reducing achievement gaps among ethnic groups and between high- and low-income students. It is administered by the private Eli and Edythe Broad Foundation.

Brown v. *Board of Education of Topeka*

The landmark 1954 U.S. Supreme Court decision that banned racially segregated schools, saying that "separate educational facilities are inherently unequal." In mandating desegregation, *Brown* v. *Board of Education* led to widespread busing and ushered in sweeping changes in education. *Brown* was brought by thirteen black parents who challenged Topeka's racially segregated schools. The plaintiffs lost in U.S. District Court, but the case was appealed to the U.S. Supreme Court, along with similar cases from Virginia, South Carolina, and Delaware. They were consolidated by the court as *Brown* v. *Board*.

Introduction to the *Brown* Decision

Today, education is perhaps the most important function of state and local governments. Compulsory school attendance laws and the great expenditures for education both demonstrate our recognition of the importance of education to our democratic society. It is required in the performance of our most basic public responsibilities, even service in the armed forces. It is the very foundation of good citizenship. Today it is a principal instrument in awakening the child to cultural values, in preparing him for later professional training, and in helping him to adjust normally to his environment. In these days, it is doubtful that any child may reasonably be expected to succeed in life if he is denied the opportunity of an education. Such an opportunity, where the state has undertaken to provide it, is a right which must be made available to all on equal terms.

—*Chief Justice Earl Warren*

Brown's legacy continues to evolve. In 2007, a divided Supreme Court ruled that student-assignment plans in the Seattle and Jefferson County, Kentucky, districts that classified all students by race, and sometimes relied on race to achieve diversity in individual schools, violated the equal-protection clause of the Constitution's 14th Amendment. The decisions raised questions about how school districts could continue to pursue integration goals. (See *busing* and *desegregation*.)

bullying

When someone seeks to intimidate or harm a peer through words or physical action. Many states and school districts have implemented policies in an effort to curb bullying. (See *cyberbullies*.)

business-education partnerships

School-reform coalitions formed by private businesses and schools or school districts. Partnerships have evolved from individual school partnerships to the introduction of management principles into public schools to a range of reform ideas, from school choice to higher performance standards, most recently focused on the systemic reform of schools.

busing

The frequently contested practice of transporting students—by bus—to a school other than the one in their neighborhood to increase racial diversity in schools, for example, by busing black children to predominantly white schools and vice versa. The U.S. Supreme Court's groundbreaking decision in *Brown* v. *Board of Education of Topeka* led to court-ordered desegregation and busing plans in many large districts in the 1960s and 1970s. In recent years, critics have sued successfully to revise such plans. In 2007, the Supreme Court ruled that student-assignment plans in the Seattle and Jefferson County, Kentucky, districts that classified all students by race, and sometimes relied on race to achieve diversity in individual schools, violated the equal-protection clause of the 14th Amendment. The Court made its ruling in *Parents Involved in Community Schools* v. *Seattle School District No. 1* and *Meredith* v. *Jefferson County Board of Education*. (See *Brown* v. *Board of Education of Topeka* and *desegregation*.)

C

Child Study Team (CST)
Teams often used by public schools to identify children with special learning needs.

career academies
Separate schools within schools that combine academic and vocational preparation. Career academies center their coursework on a single theme, such as banking or the health professions, and often maintain relationships with local businesses and employers in order to provide students with career guidance and practical experience. They play a vital role in comprehensive efforts to smooth the transition from school to work for students who do not plan to attend college.

career and technical education
Instruction that prepares a student for employment immediately after the completion of high school. Although often thought of in terms of auto shop or carpentry courses, such programs frequently also include a strong academic component and teach cutting-edge skills such as computer-aided design. Many proponents prefer "career and technical education" to the older term, "vocational education." (See *vocational education.*)

Managers Team Up to Run Charters

By Caroline Hendrie, San Diego
Education Week: *June 15, 2005*

Even before a single student had signed up for High Tech High School, the founders of the new charter school on San Diego Bay knew they didn't want that first school to be their last. To that end, leaders of the 450-student school worked with interested groups to start new schools around the country based on their distinctive small-school design. Yet after watching some schools in the far-flung network stray from the design's core principles, last year they changed course and formed a nonprofit "charter-management organization."

In opting to take the CMO route, High Tech High became part of a small but growing tribe of charter school pioneers who are trying to create not just one high-performing school but whole systems of them from scratch. At the moment, California is on the trend's leading edge, but the organizations are cropping up elsewhere as supporters of the approach push to increase the odds that success stories like High Tech High can multiply. "They're extremely important and valuable," said Deborah J. Stipek, the dean of the school of education at Stanford University and the chairwoman of the board of Leadership Public Schools, a San Francisco-based CMO. "This is a very exciting adventure in education."

Carnegie unit

A credit representing the completion of a core of high school courses. Developed in the early 1900s to set norms for curriculum and course time in public schools across the country, these are named after the Carnegie Foundation for the Advancement of Teaching, which first suggested the practice.

cash-incentive programs

Programs being tested in some school districts that pay students for academic performance. Policymakers remain strongly divided on the wisdom and long-term implications of cash-for-achievement programs.

Chance-for-Success Index

Developed by the EPE Research Center for its annual *Quality Counts* report, the index calculates the odds that a child who grows up in a particular state will perform as well as the average child in the top-ranked state on thirteen key benchmarks from birth to adulthood.

character education

Deliberate instruction in basic values and morals, ideally woven into lessons throughout the curriculum. A national movement seeks to include character education in school curricula as a means of addressing what many educators, policymakers, and community members view as a decline in values among children, particularly honesty, respect, responsibility, empathy, and civic duty.

charter management organization (CMO)

Organizations that provide administrative support and curriculum development for multiple charter schools. (See *charter schools*.)

charter schools

Schools run independently of the traditional public school system but receiving public funding. In exchange for regulatory freedom, the schools are bound to the terms of a contract or "charter" that lays out their mission, academic goals, and accountability procedures. State laws set the parameters for charter contracts, which are overseen by a designated charter school authorizer—often the local school district or related agency.

With their relative autonomy, charter schools are seen as a way to provide greater educational choice and innovation within the public school system. Their founders are often teachers, parents, or activists who feel restricted by traditional public schools. In addition, many charters are run by for-profit companies, forming a key component of the privatization movement in education. The first charter school was founded in Minnesota in 1992.

While the concept is popular with the public, some charter schools have come under fire for mismanagement and failing to boost student achievement. Unscrupulous charter operators have used the schools as a way to pocket public money. But charter schools today are a fixture of the public school choice system and highly regarded in many communities. (See *choice* and *KIPP schools*.)

Child Nutrition Act

The federal law that governs the National School Lunch Program, along with breakfast and summer food programs and the Special Supplemental Nutrition Program for Women, Infants, and Children. First enacted in 1966, the law was reauthorized in 2004 and directed school districts to enact wellness policies that include goals for nutrition education and nutritional guidelines for all food available on campuses during the school day.

Children's Internet Protection Act (CIPA)

Passed by Congress in 2000, this federal law states that school districts must protect students from harmful materials—such as pornography and obscene language—to be eligible for federal E-rate money, which can subsidize up to 90 percent of schools' telecommunications and technology costs.

choice

At its most basic and uncontroversial, school choice is a reform movement focused on affording parents the right to choose which school their child attends. That said, the concept and the issues surrounding choice are anything but uncontroversial.

Private school choice—which allows parents to use government-funded vouchers to send their children to private schools—touches on an array of tough questions about parents' and students' rights, church-state separation, and, as some people see it, the very survival of public schools. By comparison, public school choice, in its various forms, gives parents the option of transferring their children out of lower-performing public schools to higher-performing public schools. (See *charter schools, magnet school, school choice,* and *vouchers.*)

civic education

Teaching that addresses the roles and responsibilities of citizens and their governments.

cluster grouping

Grouping gifted students together within an otherwise heterogeneous class headed by a teacher who has skills and interest in working with high-achieving learners.

cognitive sciences

A relatively new area of study that focuses on how people think and learn. Research in the field cuts across a wide range of disciplines—including computer science, linguistics, anthropology, neuroscience, sociology, and psychology. Cognitive scientists question the traditional model of schooling in which teachers lecture and drill students. Rather, they say, children actively construct or make meaning of their world based on interactions with their environment.

collaboration

A partnership of professionals and community members who work together to improve the condition of children and families. Such partnerships generally involve some combination of educators, human-services professionals, community groups, parents, businesses, government officials, and neighborhood leaders.

collective bargaining

Bargaining between an employer and a group of employees. Teachers' unions typically negotiate contracts with school districts for all of their members. Collective-bargaining agreements enjoy protection under the No Child Left Behind Act, which says that districts cannot pursue options to restructure schools that conflict with existing contracts. However, the Bush administration said districts should be allowed to override the contracts in staffing their most troubled schools.

college access programs

Nonprofit organizations designed to increase the number of students who pursue education beyond high school. These organizations provide financial counseling, scholarships, career guidance, tutoring, and test preparation, and organize college visits. Through advising and financial assistance, the National College Access Network (NCAN) supports member programs that motivate students to gain access to postsecondary

Pointing the Way to College
By Alyson Klein
Education Week: *January 6, 2006*

On a recent afternoon, cousins Samantha Carter and Arielle Giles dropped by the guidance department at Nelson County High School here to show off their acceptance letters to Ferrum College, a small private school in southwestern Virginia.

Sarah Borish, who worked with both students on their applications, gave the cousins her congratulations—and an assignment: Check out Ferrum's internship opportunities, athletics, and, especially, graduation rates, particularly for students who, like the cousins, are African-Americans.

Ms. Borish, who received her bachelor's degree in history from the University of Virginia last spring, is one of more than 60 newly minted college graduates serving in the **National College Advising Corps.** The corps is a network of higher education access programs that places recent college graduates in high schools to address an information barrier that hinders many academically qualified low-income students in gaining access to college.

Ms. Giles, who has lived all her life in this farming community in the Blue Ridge Mountains and will be the first in her family to go to college, credits Ms. Borish with helping her stay on track through the application process.

continued

"If she wasn't here, I probably wouldn't have gotten anything done," Ms. Giles said.

The National College Advising Corps, which started at U.Va., was initially financed in 2004 by a two-year, $623,000 grant from the Jack Kent Cooke Foundation, a Lansdowne, Va.-based charity formed with a bequest from the late businessman who was best known as the owner of the Washington Redskins football team. Mr. Cooke died in 1997. The organization focuses on helping academically talented, financially needy students reach their potential.

education. The National College Advising Corps, based at the University of North Carolina at Chapel Hill, is a similar program that uses college advisers to augment guidance counselors' college-outreach efforts.

College Board (or College Entrance Examination Board)

The New York City–based nonprofit organization that sponsors the SAT and the Advanced Placement (AP) program, among others. The College Board is composed of colleges, universities, and other agencies and associations that offer services to secondary and postsecondary students. (See also *SAT* and *Advanced Placement*.)

college-readiness rates

Jay P. Greene and Marcus A. Winters of the Manhattan Institute for Policy Research have calculated "college-readiness rates" for each state, based on what they describe as the minimum standards of the least-selective four-year colleges. Among other criteria, the index is based on the percentages of students who graduated on time with a standard high school diploma and passed four years of English, three years of math, and two years each of science, social science, and a foreign language. Greene and Winters estimated that about 1.3 million students were college-ready in the class of 2002, a figure just under the nearly 1.4 million who had actually enrolled in college for the first time the year before.

Comer schools

Schools that adhere to a system of top-to-bottom reform developed by Yale University psychiatrist James P. Comer. Comer schools operate on the theory that children's experiences at home and in school deeply affect their social and psychological development, which in turn shapes their academic achievement. The Comer model seeks to bridge gaps—social, psychological, and cultural—between home and school. Federal researchers have found evidence that the popular model is effective.

comprehensive school reform

Comprehensive school reform, or CSR, is among the waves of improvement efforts that radiated from the 1983 report *A Nation at Risk,* a sweeping indictment of U.S. public schools. CSR focuses on improvements schoolwide, encompassing everything from curriculum to school management.

The basic principle of CSR is that instead of a fragmented approach to addressing achievement issues, schools must overhaul their systems from top to bottom. Therefore, from a CSR perspective, a rigorous curriculum program is not the only element critical to raising student-achievement levels. Rather, efficient school management, ongoing staff development, frequent student assessment, and parent involvement are also vitally important. Because the strategies of this reform movement are wide-ranging and encompass all parts of a school's operations, CSR is also referred to as "schoolwide" or "whole school" reform. (See also *ability grouping, at risk,* and *Title I.*)

computational thinking

An emerging field that draws on computer science methods and concepts to solve problems, design systems, or study human behavior. The term was coined by Jennifer Wing, head of the Computer Science Department at Carnegie Mellon University. Carnegie Mellon and Microsoft are working together to create a center to promote computational thinking in K–12 and higher education.

constructivism

Constructivist theory posits that children build new information onto preexisting notions and modify their understanding in light of new data. In the process, their ideas increase in complexity and power. Constructivist theorists dismiss the idea that students learn by absorbing information through lectures or repeated rote practice.

content management system

See *Learning Management System.*

content standards

Standards that set out what students should be expected to learn. The challenge of the standards movement lies in agreeing on what it is students should learn and setting standards that are appropriately challenging yet fair. Debates over national standards tend to be framed on one side by ideals of national consistency and equity and on the other by the authority of states and districts over the content and administration of schooling. (See also *standards*.)

cooperative education

A program that allows students to receive credit for career work undertaken in their field of study. Businesses create plans for training and evaluation of students in cooperative, or *co-op,* programs.

cooperative learning

A method of instruction that encourages students to work in small groups, learning material and then presenting what they have learned to other small groups. In doing so, they take responsibility for their own learning as well as that of their classmates.

Market for K–12 Course-Management Systems Expands

By Andrew Trotter
Education Week: *February 27, 2008*

Eighth grade teacher Molly Tipton of El Paso, Texas, is part of a growing number of K–12 educators in regular classrooms who are using **course-management systems** to share assignments, homework, classroom assessments, and other information with students and their parents. A course-management system is a software program that allows controlled exchanges via the Internet of just about any kind of information related to a course, although the features of individual products differ. Through Moodle, an online CMS, Ms. Tipton now posts reading passages and links to Web sites that are related to her lessons. She also has set up a popular online chat room for her students and posts homework assignments online, a feature that students as well as some parents have embraced. Moodle's online capabilities, she said, are making her social studies classes a hybrid between traditional and online courses.

core subjects

Subject areas deemed to be critical areas of learning. Typically, the list of core subjects includes English reading or language arts, mathematics, science, history, government and civics, and arts.

corporal punishment

A traditional method of physically disciplining students; the term usually refers to paddling. A 2008 report by Human Rights Watch and the American Civil Liberties Union found twenty-one states permitted corporal punishment. The study's authors wrote that males, black students, and students in special education were far more likely to be paddled than other students.

co-teaching

A model of teaching frequently used with students with

disabilities. Co-teaching takes place when a general education teacher and a special educator collaborate on lesson- and activity-planning activities and work together in the same classroom to instruct students with and without disabilities.

course-management system

Software that makes it possible to share information related to a course over the Internet. Many K–12 educators are beginning to use course-management systems to share assignments, assessments, and other information with students and their parents. Such a system allows educators to post materials on the Web without having to know computer languages.

creationism

Creationism is the product of a literal interpretation of the Biblical story of Genesis and holds that God created the world in a single act approximately six thousand years ago. To many creationists, the theory of evolution is heresy, and some have sought to have the related theory of "intelligent design" taught in schools alongside evolution. (See also *evolution* and *intelligent design.*)

Creative Commons

A nonprofit organization that licenses creative works (including some teaching tools) for free, limited use. The organization's goal is to protect developers while enabling limited free use of their materials.

credit recovery

Initiatives designed to allow high school students in danger of dropping out to make up the academic credits they need to earn a diploma. Today, some high schools are turning to online courses to help faltering students revive their academic careers and retrieve the credits they need to earn their diplomas.

criterion-referenced test

A standardized test that is aligned with a state's academic standards and thus intended primarily to measure students' performance with respect to those standards rather than to the performance of their peers nationally. (See also *norm-referenced test.*)

critical literacy

The ability to engage in reading with a critical eye. It takes reading beyond simply decoding the sounds within a word to a deeper comprehension that involves being able to ask questions about what a text says about the world or the subject at hand. The International Reading Association calls critical literacy a goal of reading instruction.

critical thinking

The mental process of acquiring information, then evaluating it to reach a logical conclusion or answer. Increasingly, educators believe that schools should focus more on critical thinking than on memorization of facts.

cultural literacy

The central theory of E.D. Hirsch Jr.'s widely debated 1987 book, *Cultural Literacy: What Every American Needs to Know,* which put forth the theory that literate Americans share a core body of knowledge that can be catalogued and taught.

curriculum

The subject matter that teachers and students cover in class.

curriculum compacting

The streamlining of material for gifted students. The process also involves documenting student proficiency, setting goals, and enumerating specific enrichment activities geared to the students involved. The curriculum compacting practice was developed by Joseph Renzulli and Linda Smith in 1978.

curriculum mapping

A process of collecting and using data on teaching and learning in a particular class, grade, or school to plan out a coordinated, effective curriculum, across the school year or a designated period of time. Maps can be revised as new data becomes available.

cyberbullies

Individuals who attempt to intimidate or denigrate others online through harassing or vulgar e-mails or spreading gossip or secrets about others through e-mail and online social-networking sites. (See *bullying.*)

D

data-based decision making

The proliferation of local and state testing has generated enormous amounts of data about student achievement, which school leaders are now being asked to take into account when making decisions. The test information is just one kind of data now at the fingertips of school leaders: they also have access to data generated by periodic classroom tests or by assessments conducted by teachers of early literacy, for example. The idea is for educators to examine this data and use it to set priorities, and then to recheck to ensure that schools are aligned for success.

Data Quality Campaign

This Austin, Texas-based organization was established in 2006 to call more attention to the issue of data collection by districts and states and to improve the quality of the data. The Data Quality Campaign focuses mostly on state data systems, and a progress report from the organization released in November 2007 found that states are moving forward. The report found that forty-seven states had data systems in place that included five or more of the ten essential elements for success identified by the organization. Among those elements are the ability to track student test scores from year to year; an individual student-identification system; information on student enrollment and demographics; the ability to provide information on untested students and the reasons they were not tested; student-level college readiness test scores; and the ability to match students with their teachers.

decentralization

The breakup and distribution of power from a central government authority, usually including a reduction of the personnel and funding of that authority. In education, the term is most frequently used to describe the transfer of school policymaking authority from the federal to the state level, or the transfer of decision-making authority from the state level to districts or schools.

decoding

Deciphering the sounds of individual letters in a word and then putting those sounds together to read the word in full. In essence, sounding things out, or phonics. (See also *critical literacy* and *phonics.*)

Department of Defense Education Activity

The civilian agency within the U.S. Department of Defense that oversees the network of schools—overseas and domestic—on U.S. military bases.

desegregation

Efforts aimed at reducing racial isolation in schools and improving racial balance. Desegregation got its start with the U.S. Supreme Court's landmark ruling in 1954 in *Brown* v. *Board of Education of Topeka,* in which a group of parents challenged the practice of sending children to racially segregated schools in many Southern states.

The desegregation movement has weathered many challenges and evolved to include voluntary desegregation tools such as magnet schools within predominantly minority-attended schools. In 2007, the Supreme Court ruled that student-assignment plans in the Seattle and Jefferson County, Kentucky, districts that classified all students by race, and sometimes relied on race to achieve diversity in individual schools, violated the equal-protection clause of the 14th Amendment. The Court handed down its decision in the cases *Parents Involved in Community Schools* v. *Seattle School District No. 1* and *Meredith* v. *Jefferson County Board of Education.* (See *Brown* v. *Board of Education* and *busing.*)

(John) Dewey

One of the late nineteenth and early twentieth centuries' leading thinkers and writers on education.

Still influential today, John Dewey (1859–1952) believed that people learn by putting thought into action: primarily, by confronting problems that arise while engaging in activities that interest them. He advocated that education start with a child's interest in concrete, everyday experiences and build on that understanding to connect with more formal subject matter. At the Laboratory School of the University of Chicago—a school Dewey founded in 1896—children participated in experiences drawn from community life and occupations.

Dewey also saw schools as engines of democracy in which children would learn citizenship through practice. In them, children would form the habits of mind that would enable them not only to live in society but also to improve it. In 1899, his first major book on education, *The School and Society,* attempted to spell out the relationship between the education of the young and the development of an intelligent citizenry.

> **Extract from "My Pedagogic Creed"**
>
> I believe that the school is primarily a social institution. Education being a social process, the school is simply that form of community life in which all those agencies are concentrated that will be most effective in bringing the child to share in the inherited resources of the race, and to use his own powers for social ends.
>
> *John Dewey, in* The School Journal, *January 16, 1897*

diagnostic assessment

Also known as preassessments, diagnostic assessments are used to determine what a student knows about a subject before that subject is taught.

differentiated instruction

Teaching students at different levels of skill and knowledge in the same classroom by means of strategies such as giving them different work, varying the type of questions asked them, and putting them in groups that change as frequently as daily.

Differential Abilities Scales (DAS)

A standardized test designed to measure students' strengths and weaknesses.

Digest of Education Statistics

Annual report produced by the U.S. Department of Education's Institute of Education Sciences. The digest covers prekindergarten through graduate school and includes a wide array of data, including the number of schools and colleges, students, teachers, and graduates.

digital divide

The term *digital divide* was coined in the U.S. Department of Commerce report "Falling Through the Net." It described the gap between the technological haves and have-nots. More recently, rather than referring to the presence or absence of technology, the term speaks to the disparity in how technology is used in schools.

diploma

The certificate earned at the successful completion of high school or college. Earning a standard high school diploma demands different levels of performance in high school coursework across the states. Requirements vary both in the total number of courses students must complete to qualify for a standard diploma and in the distribution of those courses across academic disciplines. To encourage and reward students who exceed standard requirements, some states award advanced diplomas or some type of formal recognition for additional or more rigorous coursework and other accomplishments

Direct Instruction

"Direct Instruction"—with its first letters capitalized—is the proper name of a widely used skills-based instruction program developed in the 1960s by Siegfried Engelmann and Wesley Becker. It involves carefully scripted lesson plans and spans a wide range of subjects and grade levels. Direct Instruction began as a reading and mathematics program for children in kindergarten through third grade; it was known then as DISTAR, or Direct Instructional System for Teaching and Remediation. The Direct Instruction program has been criticized by many educators and academics for its lockstep structure.

By comparison, "direct instruction"—with lowercase first letters—is a more general term referring to teacher-directed instruction and encompassing a variety of techniques.

direct-lending program

A financial aid program administered by the U.S. Department of Education. The program provides students with loans for higher education through the institution they attend, rather than through private lending institutions.

disability categories

The Individuals with Disabilities Education Act spells out thirteen disabilities that may qualify a student for special services in cases where the disabilities impede educational performance: autism, deafness, deaf-blindness, emotional disturbance, hearing impairment (which has a separate definition from deafness), mental retardation, multiple disabilities, orthopedic impairment, other health impairments, specific learning disabilities, speech impairments, traumatic brain injury, and visual impairments including blindness.

disaggregated data

The practice of examining students' achievement data or test scores by separating out data for specific groups. For instance, data could be disaggregated by gender, socioeconomic status, race and ethnicity, or special education, among other factors.

dispositions

Generally defined as patterns of behavior, the concept of teacher dispositions is a matter of some controversy in the teacher-educator community. In 2007, the National Council for Accreditation of Teacher Education (NCATE) changed its definition of dispositions in response to concerns and defined professional dispositions as "professional attitudes, values, and beliefs demonstrated through both verbal and nonverbal behaviors as educators interact with students, families, colleagues, and communities." The definition focuses on two dispositions in particular that it expects teacher-candidates to demonstrate: fairness and the belief that all students can learn.

disproportionality

When students of a particular population or demographic group are over- or underrepresented in special or gifted education programs relative to their group's presence in the overall student population. Many states are trying to address an overrepresentation of black male students in special education, or an underrepresentation of non-Asian ethnic minorities in gifted education.

distance learning

The use of telecommunications technologies, including satellites, telephones, and cable-television systems, to broadcast instruction from one central site to one or more remote locations. Typically, a television image of a teacher is broadcast to students in remote locations. This may also be done using interactive videoconferencing. School districts frequently use distance learning so a teacher can teach to students in more than one school at a time. Rural districts often rely on distance learning. (See *e-learning*.)

distributed leadership

The formal and informal networks in schools that determine which people are influential, whether by virtue of their position or of their reputation with their peers. Interest in the idea stems from a recognition that principals' jobs are frequently too big and leave too little time for them to pay close attention to the quality of instruction. Some states have sought to encourage a distribution of leadership by creating career ladders that allow teachers to take on roles outside the classroom.

drug-free school zones

In response to public concern over an increase in illegal drug use during the 1980s, the U.S. Congress and many state legislatures have passed laws designating areas around schools as drug-free zones. Anyone convicted of possession or use of illegal drugs in these areas is subject to increased penalties under the law. The actual area of a zone and the penalties attached to it vary from state to state.

dual enrollment

Courses that allow high school students to receive both high school and college credit simultaneously fall under the broad definition of dual enrollment. In addition to concurrent enrollment, examples include tech-prep, which generally serves students in career and technical education, and early-college high schools, usually located on college campuses, which allow students to work toward an associate's degree, or two years of college credit. They can be offered at colleges, taught by professors, and attended by a mix of high school and college students. And many experts consider Advanced Placement courses a dual-enrollment option, since students who receive qualifying scores on the AP exams have the opportunity to earn college credit for courses taken in high school. (See also *Advanced Placement*.)

dual-immersion or dual-language

See *two-way bilingual education*.

due process
See *Individuals with Disabilities Education Act.*

Dynamic Indicators of Basic Early Literacy Skills (DIBELS)
An assessment tool developed by researchers at the University of Oregon and approved for use under the federal Reading First program in states to monitor student progress on reading fluency and other measures. DIBELS faced controversy after the U.S. Department of Education's inspector general found that the Education Department appeared to promote DIBELS over other assessments during workshops for state officials and suggested that a federal contractor did not appropriately screen consultants, some of whom had financial ties to DIBELS, for conflicts of interest.

dyscalculia
A learning disability that causes severe difficulties in learning mathematics.

dysgraphia
A learning disability in which individuals have great difficulty expressing themselves in writing.

dyslexia
A reading impairment, thought to be a genetic condition, that affects up to 10 percent of the nation's schoolchildren. One trait of dyslexia might be transposing letters. Children born to parents with dyslexia may be eight times as likely as the general population to have the condition.

E

Early Childhood Longitudinal Study

A federal study that tracks two groups of young children: one from birth to kindergarten and the other from kindergarten through eighth grade. Administered by the National Center for Education Statistics, the study offers data on children's transition to school and their growth through eighth grade.

EdisonLearning

A private, for-profit company that manages public schools. Formerly Edison Schools Inc., the for-profit company says it served more than 285,000 public school students in nineteen states, the District of Columbia, and the United Kingdom in the 2006–07 school year. EdisonLearning has weathered rocky financial terrain, criticism of its management style, and questions about its accomplishments since its launch in 1992. The company changed its name to EdisonLearning in 2008 and announced that it was expanding into online learning.

Education for All Handicapped Children Act

The original name of the federal Individuals with Disabilities Education Act. President Gerald Ford signed the Education for All Handicapped Children Act into law in 1975. Its goal was to establish a national system of special education and bring previously excluded children into the nation's schools. (See *Individuals with Disabilities Education Act.*)

educational management organization (EMO)

A type of organization contracted to operate, start up, or provide comprehensive instructional and management services to schools.

Education Reform Network

A communications network connecting schools, educators, and education advocates to share ideas and new approaches to improve teaching and learning and to discuss education reform topics. The Eisenhower Regional Alliance for Mathematics and Science Education Reform introduced the service.

Education Resources Information Center (ERIC)

A federal database run by the U.S. Department of Education's Institute of Education Sciences. Available on the Internet at http://eric.ed.gov, ERIC enables researchers and other interested individuals to search more than 1 million bibliographic records of journal articles and other education materials, including full text of some materials.

Education Sciences Reform Act (ESRA)

Federal law that created the Institute of Education Sciences, the research arm of the U.S. Department of Education.

Educational Testing Service (ETS)

Nonprofit corporation that produces and administers the SAT college-entrance and the Praxis teacher-certification examinations, among others. (See *Praxis* and *SAT.*)

edutainment

A general classification for software that combines elements of instruction and entertainment, including video, animation, and music. Educators disagree on the educational value of most edutainment software.

e-learning

E-learning includes virtual classrooms, Internet-based elementary through high school courses, professional development courses, and online testing programs. (See also *distance learning.*)

Elementary and Secondary Education Act (ESEA)

Passed in 1965 as part of President Lyndon Johnson's War on Poverty, the law authorizes the federal government's single largest investment in elementary and secondary education. The Elementary and Secondary Education Act (ESEA) focuses on children from high-poverty communities and students at risk of educational failure. The act authorizes several well-known federal education programs, including Title I, Safe and Drug-Free Schools, Bilingual Education (Title VII), and Impact Aid. Congress had reauthorized the law eight times as of 2008. (In reauthorizing a law, Congress keeps the legislation active rather than allowing it to phase out.) In 2002, Congress amended ESEA and reauthorized it as the No Child Left Behind Act. (See *No Child Left Behind Act.*)

emotional and behavioral disorders

Also called EBDs, emotional and behavioral disorders are characterized by consistently aggressive, impulsive, or withdrawn behavior, including schizophrenia. Each state classifies these conditions differently. Clinicians generally consider a behavior to be an EBD if it impairs personal, social, academic, and vocational skills.

English as a second language (ESL)

Broad category of instruction for English-language learners that may focus on English immersion, but also may include some support to individuals in their native tongue. Typically, classes are made up of

Instructional Model May Yield Gains for English-Learners

By Mary Ann Zehr, New York Education Week: *December 5, 2007*

Educators at a small public school for immigrant students at the foot of the Manhattan Bridge here believe its unusual instructional approach—which includes mixing students at various levels of English proficiency—is a key reason why Brooklyn International High School has a graduation rate that outpaces that of many other public schools in New York City. Eighty percent of its students graduate after four years, while, on average, 60 percent of New York City's students do the same. Particularly impressive is the school's success with English-language learners. The four-year high school graduation rate in 2007 for students who were still ELLs at graduation was 65 percent; in 2006, the most recent year for which data are available, the city's average four-year graduation rate for ELLs was 26 percent. Experts on **ELLs** sound a note of caution, however. They say that teaching ELLs in groups with mixed levels of English fluency can be effective, but that schools must have a strong professional-development program to prepare teachers to deliver differentiated instruction.

students who speak many different languages but are not fluent in English. They may attend classes for only a period a day, to work strictly on English skills, or attend for a full day and focus both on academics and English.

English immersion

Instruction for English-language learners that is delivered entirely in English. Teachers strive to deliver lessons in simplified English so that students learn English and academic subjects at the same time.

English-language learners

Students enrolled in U.S. schools who speak a language other than English and haven't yet mastered English. They are also known as limited-English-proficient (LEP) students, and may be either immigrants or children born in the United States. Each state has a different way of ascertaining whether a child is an English-language learner (ELL). Usually such students receive bilingual education or ESL services.

enrichment

Enrichment programs—originally designed primarily for gifted students, but now widely used with at-risk children as well—are intended to supplement the regular academic curriculum for students who might otherwise be bored with their classwork. For the gifted, they are an alternative to acceleration, so that even the most able students can remain in class with children their own age and maturity, yet be adequately challenged. Sometimes run as pull-out programs, enrichment programs are also an alternative to creating entirely separate gifted classrooms. Enrichment is intended to add value to the curriculum, often in an enjoyable way, through such activities as special projects, guest speakers, concerts, and museum visits. Many educators have found that what was originally considered enrichment is actually worth incorporating into the regular curriculum.

environmental education

Efforts to teach about ecosystems and the environment, and how changes in them can affect the health and survival of people, other species, and natural resources.

equity

Fairness or justice, usually referring to the equitable distribution of something valued. In the education field, this term refers to the fair

distribution of funding, technology, facilities, services, and equal
education opportunities for both male and female students, as well as
students of different races and ethnicities, students with disabilities,
students with limited proficiency in English, and students in high-
poverty schools.

E-rate

The E-rate (short for education rate) is a program administered by the
Federal Communications Commission that pays for telecommunications
services and related equipment for the nation's K–12 schools and public
libraries. The FCC began awarding E-rate aid in 1998.

ESEA

See *Elementary and Secondary Education Act* and *No Child Left
Behind Act.*

ESL

English as a second language. Refers to students who are not native
speakers of English or programs pertaining to the teaching of those
students. (See *bilingual education* and *Limited-English-Proficient
students.*)

evidence-based education movement

A campaign to transform education into a field where policymakers and
educators routinely rely on rigorous research, much as medical doctors
do, to choose the programs and practices they put in schools.

evolution

Made famous by British naturalist Charles Darwin, the theory of
evolution holds that species evolve through natural selection and
random mutation, and that the evolutionary process began billions
of years ago. Evolution is taught in schools across the United States
and around the globe. Scientists say evidence supporting the theory
of evolution includes fossil records, the existence of similar structures
in different animals, and the fact that all living things share similar
biochemistry. They say the theory of evolution is not just scientifically valid, it is the unifying theory of biology. Advocates of what is
called "intelligent design" disagree, however, and argue that teachers should emphasize that evolution is a theory, not fact, and that
intelligent design should be taught in schools as well. (See *intelligent
design.*)

exit exam

A high-stakes test that students are required to pass to earn a diploma. Many states have adopted exit exams to ensure that all high school graduates have achieved basic levels of academic proficiency and are ready for college or the workforce. Opponents worry that the exams will encourage struggling students to drop out of school, while others dispute any evidence that exit exams have had a negative impact on graduation rates. (See also *high-stakes testing*.)

Expeditionary Learning/Outward Bound

The program, based in New York, makes real-world instruction and community-service projects a key feature of school curricula. Although the Outward Bound outdoor-adventure program came to the United States in 1962, it did not evolve into a formal whole-school-improvement program until 1992. In 2003, the Bill and Melinda Gates Foundation awarded Expeditionary Learning a five-year, $12.6 million grant to create twenty small college-preparatory high schools.

experiential education

Education that stresses hands-on experience, accomplished by field trips, internships, or activity-oriented projects, as opposed to traditional classroom learning.

F

facilitated communication

A form of augmentative and alternative communication (AAC). The technique involves training an autistic or nonverbal person to use a keyboard or to communicate by pointing at letters, pictures, or symbols. Originally hailed as a breakthrough, facilitated communication has also faced deep skepticism. A number of researchers have found that facilitators were guiding the hands of people with autism or other disorders.

Family Educational Rights and Privacy Act (FERPA)

The federal law that protects the privacy of student records in schools receiving federal funding. Under the law, schools must obtain written permission from parents or eligible students to release student education records in most instances. FERPA also grants parents and eligible students—those eighteen or over, or attending school beyond the high school level—certain rights, including the right to request and review a student's educational records.

family literacy

Programs that involve parents, children, and extended family members in ways of using literacy at home.

finance equity

See *school finance*.

financial aid

Monetary assistance available to students attending institutions of higher education. That aid can consist of low-interest loans, needs-based grants, scholarships, work-study funds, and fellowships, in any combination.

formative assessment

An assessment designed to gauge the progress of students' learning while teaching and learning are still under way. The aim of formative assessment is to guide teaching and learning for teachers and students.

fourth grade slump

For some pupils, reading ability starts a dramatic downhill slide right around fourth grade. Researchers say the phenomenon tends to occur when reading instruction shifts from basic decoding and word recognition to development of fluency and comprehension, which often comes in fourth grade. The term is attributed to the late Jeanne S. Chall, a professor and educational psychologist at Harvard University's graduate school of education, who was one of the nation's foremost experts on reading.

free, appropriate public education (FAPE)

The Individuals with Disabilities Education Act guarantees all students with disabilities a "free, appropriate public education." The term is frequently abbreviated as FAPE. If students cannot be served adequately in the public schools, under the terms of FAPE, school systems must pay the cost of educating children with special needs at a facility that will accommodate their learning needs.

free schools

Small, private—and controversial—alternative schools that have rejected standards-based education and instead consider themselves learner-based environments. One of the oldest and most celebrated free schools is Summerhill, a boarding school in Leiston, England. It first opened in 1921.

(Bill & Melinda) Gates Foundation

The world's largest charitable foundation. Created by Microsoft founder Bill Gates and his wife, Melinda, the foundation has become a major donor to education and schools. Among its goals is helping "ensure that 80 percent of high school graduate college-ready, with a focus on low-income and minority people reaching this target." (Editor's note: The Gates Foundation provides grant underwriting to Editorial Projects in Education, the nonprofit parent company of Education Week Press.)

gender bias

Conscious or unconscious differential treatment—in a textbook or by a teacher or employer—of females and males based on their sex. The bias can be subtle or overt. In education, gender bias is seen as a factor in the relative paucity of girls pursuing study in mathematics and science. While both boys and girls tend to lose interest in math and science as they move from elementary to high school, females' interest and confidence falls off more sharply, according to data from the National Center for Education Statistics, an arm of the U.S. Department of Education. Research on gender differences in students' math and science achievement and motivation received considerable attention in the 1980s, and recent years have seen a resurgence in interest, possibly because of increasing concerns about the shortage of students, especially women, entering technical, engineering, and other such fields.

GED (General Educational Development)
A GED certificate is the equivalent of a high school diploma. GED tests are designed to measure the academic skills and knowledge expected of high school graduates in the United States and Canada and can be earned by students who drop out of high school. According to the American Council on Education, the first GED tests were developed in 1942 to help veterans resume their education after returning from World War II.

geocoding
The practice of assigning geographic identifiers to students so that analysts can gather income information from the U.S. Census Bureau about the areas in which the children live.

gifted students
Pupils who are considered to have the capacity to achieve beyond the norm because of their IQ scores, their demonstrated ability in the classroom, or both. Once limited to academic skills, the definition of giftedness in many schools is expanding to include children with a wide variety of talents. (See also *IQ*.)

Government Accountability Office (GAO)
The watchdog agency of Congress. The office is charged with auditing and evaluating federal programs, including federally funded education programs.

GPA
Common abbreviation for grade point average.

Graduation Counts Compact
Signed by the governors of all fifty states in 2005, the Compact was intended as an impetus to states to produce more realistic and consistent graduation rates. The Compact requires states to work toward implementing a graduation rate calculation that tracks individual students from ninth grade to graduation and accounts for transfers in and out of the system. But, as of mid-2008, the National Governors Association reported that only sixteen states were calculating and publicly reporting a graduation rate consistent with the formula to which the states had agreed three years earlier.

graphing calculator

Frequently described as a cross between a traditional electronic calculator and a microcomputer, a graphing calculator allows users to graph equations, at the touch of a button, that otherwise would take hours of pencil-and-paper work to understand. Many schools require graphing calculators for certain math classes.

growth models

An accountability system based on the academic growth students show from year to year. With growth models, schools can receive credit for students who make progress over the course of the year, even if they have not reached the proficient level in achievement.

Hazelwood School District v. Kuhlmeier

The U.S. Supreme Court's 1988 ruling in *Hazelwood* authorized school administrators to supervise the content of official high school newspapers. The court held that school authorities do not violate the First Amendment rights of students by controlling the content of student publications if the officials' actions are reasonably related to legitimate pedagogical concerns. This standard differed from that applied to non-disruptive student speech to protest the Vietnam War addressed in a prior case, *Tinker* v. *Des Moines Independent Community School District.* (See *Tinker* v. *Des Moines Independent Community School District.*)

Head Start

First launched in 1965 as part of President Lyndon Johnson's War on Poverty, this federal program provides economically deprived preschoolers with education, nutrition, health, and social services at special centers based in schools and community settings throughout the country. The program, designed to help prepare disadvantaged children for school, is known for its high degree of parental involvement in planning and management.

Health Information Privacy Protection Act (HIPPA)

The federal law requiring that student health information collected by districts be kept private.

Hendrick Hudson Central School District Board of Education v. Rowley

The first Supreme Court decision related to the Education for All Handicapped Children Act of 1975, the precursor to the Individuals with Disabilities Education Act. The court's 1982 ruling in the case held that states and districts need not provide children with disabilities the "best" education available, but that they must follow the procedures set forth in the special education law and provide an educational plan that is reasonably calculated to enable the child to receive education benefits. (See *Individuals with Disabilities Education Act.*)

higher-order thinking skills

Based on Bloom's Taxonomy, higher-order thinking skills are those that involve an ability to think and evaluate complex ideas. Many schools promote the teaching of higher-order thinking skills as an educational objective. (See *Bloom's Taxonomy.*)

Higher Education Act (HEA)

The law that governs a broad swath of federal higher education programs. The law was renewed most recently in 2008; the updated version of the HEA included language to promote accountability for higher education programs that prepare teachers. The law also simplified the main federal student-aid application, reducing it from seven to three pages, and altered eligibility and evaluation standards for certain federal college-access programs known as TRIO programs. (See also *TRIO programs.*)

highly qualified teachers

The federal No Child Left Behind Act of 2001 required that by the end of the 2005–06 school year, every teacher working in a public school must be "highly qualified"—meaning that a teacher is certified and has demonstrated proficiency in his or her subject matter by having majored in the subject in college or holding coursework credits equivalent to a major, passing a subject-knowledge test, or obtaining advanced certification in the subject. The law also calls for strengthening teacher preparation and professional development services. (See *in-service training* and *No Child Left Behind Act.*)

High/Scope Perry Preschool Project

Perhaps the best-known study of the long-term effects of a high-quality prekindergarten education. The High/Scope Educational

Research Foundation tracked, from age three or four through age forty for some participants, a group of 123 African Americans who were living in poverty at the start of the study. The study found that those adults who had been enrolled in preschool in their early childhood were more likely to have earned a high school diploma, more likely to hold a job and to earn more income, and less likely to have committed a crime than their counterparts who did not go to preschool.

high-stakes testing

Testing with serious consequences for students. A graduation or exit exam that high school students are required to pass in order to graduate is an example of a high-stakes test. High-stakes testing is a flashpoint topic for many in education. Some see high-stakes tests as an integral facet of the larger accountability movement while others say such testing puts unreasonable pressure on students, teachers, and schools and does not improve achievement overall.

High Schools That Work

A popular school improvement initiative that combines a rigorous academic core—at least four years of college-preparatory English and mathematics, three years of lab sciences and social studies, and one computer course—with at least four credits in a career and technical area. It was developed by the Southern Regional Education Board (SREB). In 2008, more than twelve hundred sites in thirty-two states used the High Schools That Work framework, according to the SREB.

Historically Black Colleges and Universities (HBCUs)

The Higher Education Act of 1965, as amended, defines an HBCU as "any historically black college or university that was established prior to 1964, whose principal mission was, and is, the education of black Americans, and that is accredited by a nationally recognized accrediting agency or association." Among the nation's HBCUs are Alabama A&M University, Albany State University, Alcorn State University, Benedict College, Bethune-Cookman College, Cheyney University of Pennsylvania, Fisk University, Florida A&M University, Howard University, Jackson State University, Meharry Medical College, Morgan State University, Spelman College, Virginia State University, and Wiley College. While HBCUs make up only 3 percent of America's 4,084 higher education institutions, they enroll 14 percent of all African American students in higher education.

home schooling

The practice of parents' teaching their children at home rather than sending them to public school. Methods of home schooling vary widely, ranging from following an established online curriculum to unstructured or student-driven learning. According to the U.S. Department of Education, an estimated 1.1 million students were home schooled in 2003.

High Objective Uniform State Standard of Evaluation (HOUSSE)

A provision in the No Child Left Behind Act. HOUSSE says states may create methods for veteran teachers to be deemed "highly qualified" without having to take a test or return to college. Because states have chosen different paths for making the highly qualified designation, standards differ in the degree to which teachers receive credit for their years of experience on the job rather than by measures aimed more directly at assessing their knowledge and teaching skills. A 2007 study commissioned by the U.S. Department of Education found that the standard for being "highly qualified" often differed between schools with high concentrations of poor students and better-off schools.

Horatio Alger Association of Distinguished Americans

This Washington, D.C.-based organization has released an annual report titled "State of Our Nation's Youth" since 1999.

I

illiteracy

The condition of being unable to read. People were once considered illiterate if they could not sign their name. More recently, the definition has been expanded so that literacy tests now measure people's ability to perform everyday tasks, such as understanding a bus schedule.

impact aid

Payments by Congress to school districts where the local budget and enrollment is affected by the federal government's presence. For example, the government provides impact aid to districts that draw children from areas not subject to local taxes, such as military bases or Indian reservations.

in loco parentis

A Latin phrase meaning "in place of a parent." The term often refers to educators or schools in their role of caring for children during the school day, and can feature in lawsuits based on that activity.

in need of improvement

Under the terms of the No Child Left Behind Act, a school that fails to make adequate yearly progress (AYP) for two consecutive years is considered to be "in need of improvement." The school must offer all students the opportunity to transfer to another school in the district that is reaching its AYP goals. To move out of the category, a school must meet its AYP goals for two consecutive years. (See *No Child Left Behind Act.*)

inclusion

The controversial practice—sometimes called "full inclusion"—of educating children with disabilities alongside their nondisabled peers, often in a regular classroom in their neighborhood school. The Individuals with Disabilities Education Act requires that disabled children be educated in the "least restrictive environment" possible. The practice was previously known as "mainstreaming."

independent school

A private or nonpublic school that is not part of a school system. An independent school is governed by a board of trustees instead of by its state board of education. It is funded by tuition and private donations and grants. The school must hold a nonprofit status and be accredited by an approved state or regional association. It must also be nondiscriminatory, though it can be either religious or nonreligious. (See *private school.*)

Individuals with Disabilities Education Act (IDEA)

A landmark federal law, renamed in 1997, that was originally passed as the Education for All Handicapped Children Act of 1975. In exchange for federal money, schools must guarantee that all children with disabilities receive a "free, appropriate public education." Different portions of the law cover children from birth to age twenty-one. The law has been amended several times but originally addressed children with disabilities who were kept out of the public schools and taught either at home or institutions. (See also *Section 504 of the Rehabilitation Act of 1973.*)

IDEA & Due Process

In the **Individuals with Disabilities Education Act**, due process refers to a number of rights that are guaranteed to qualified students, including the right to be evaluated, to be educated in the **least restrictive environment (LRE)**, the guarantee of a free, **appropriate public education (FAPE)**, and a parent's right to take any dispute with a school to a third party. In the event of a dispute between parents and schools over a student's placement or status under IDEA, the law states that the student will "stay put" in his or her current placement until the dispute is resolved. The so-called stay-put provision is designed to support continuity in a student's education.

individualized education program (IEP)

The individualized education program (IEP) is the educational blueprint agreed on by parents and educators for a student with disabilities. Before an IEP is developed, a student must be evaluated to determine if a disability is affecting his or her ability to learn. The school must also assemble an IEP team that includes the child's parents or guardians, a special education teacher, at least one regular education teacher, a school or district representative who is knowledgeable of resources available to the child, and someone—often a school psychologist—who can interpret the evaluation results. Parents are considered equal partners in the process. Plans are also changed as students' needs change. IEPs can include specific accommodations to students to keep them in regular education classrooms as much as possible; in some cases where schools cannot serve a child adequately, an IEP can order that the public school pay the cost to send a child to a private school that can serve the child's needs.

induction

Hands-on training for new teachers under the guidance of a more experienced mentor teacher. Induction is seen as a way of training teachers to become more effective and engaged in their jobs, thus keeping new teachers in the profession.

in-service training

The workshops and lectures designed to keep teachers abreast of the latest developments in their field. The training is called "in-service" to distinguish it from "pre-service" training, which means undergraduate coursework taken by those intending to teach. (See *highly qualified teacher.*)

instructional coach

A teacher in a full- or part-time position who works with colleagues individually and in groups to improve their teaching practice.

instructional leadership or learning-centered leadership

In an age of accountability, the terms reflect the conviction that principals and not just classroom teachers must be concerned with instruction and student achievement. Principals are to set the academic tone for the school and organize and manage their staffs for student success, rather than spending most of their time managing the building, dealing with discipline, and handling other administrative tasks.

instructional technology

Broad category of technology designed for teaching and learning. Instructional technology specialists are educators tasked with helping other teachers with the technical aspects of integrating technology into learning.

intelligent design

Intelligent design is the belief that the complexity of organisms, including human beings, suggests that their development was guided by an unnamed creator or designer. That view contrasts with the theory of evolution as advanced in the mid-nineteenth century by the British naturalist Charles Darwin, who concluded that species evolve through natural selection and random mutation. In late 2005, a federal judge in Pennsylvania issued a key opinion in *Kitzmiller* v. *Dover Area School District* declaring that intelligent design is not science, but rather a descendant of creationism. The judge said the Dover, Pennsylvania, school district's policy mandating that students be exposed to intelligent design was unconstitutional. (See also *creationism* and *evolution*.)

U.S. Judge Rules Intelligent Design Has No Place in Science Classrooms

By Sean Cavanagh
Education Week: *December 20, 2005*

In a sweeping, often acerbically worded 139-page ruling released Dec. 20, 2005, U.S. District Court Judge John E. Jones III concluded that school board members in Dover, Pa., had religious motivations in approving a district policy requiring that high school students be introduced to the **intelligent design** concept as an alternative to the theory of evolution. "We have addressed the seminal question of whether ID is science," the judge wrote in his opinion, referring to intelligent design. "We have concluded that it is not, and moreover, that ID cannot uncouple itself from its creationist, and thus religious, antecedents." While the decision has legal standing only in the jurisdiction where it was issued—the U.S. District Court for the Middle District of Pennsylvania—legal observers have said they expect it to influence similar court cases as well as decisions by local school districts in other parts of the country.

interactive whiteboard

A large wall screen that accepts projected computer images and acts as an input device, allowing teachers to draw on the screen to emphasize a point or pull pictures or other graphics from the Internet.

International Baccalaureate (IB)

The International Baccalaureate is a program of rigorous coursework and examinations based on an internationally developed curriculum. Like Advanced Placement courses, completed IB coursework often can be used to earn college credits. (See also *Advanced Placement*.)

Institute of Education Sciences

The research arm of the U.S. Department of Education.

intellectual disability

The preferred term for the condition traditionally called mental retardation. The American Association on Intellectual and Developmental Disabilities defines an intellectual disability as "a disability characterized by significant limitations both in intellectual functioning and in adaptive behavior as expressed in conceptual, social, and practical adaptive skills." Such a disability originates before the age of eighteen.

With World Growing Smaller, IB Gets Big

By Scott J. Cech
Education Week: *October 31, 2007*

The perception that the Geneva, Switzerland-based International Baccalaureate Organization's academic programs offer just what American students need in today's more globally competitive environment seems to be catching on. After decades of obscurity and slow expansion, the pace of growth in **International Baccalaureate** programs—including courses of study for the primary and middle school years as well as the better-known high-school-level programs—has quickened considerably. Favorable word of mouth among educators—along with an endorsement from President Bush and glowing accounts in national magazines—has helped catapult IB into U.S. classrooms. More than 225 American schools so far [2007] have started offering at least one IB program, bringing the U.S. total to 800. The process of becoming IB-authorized and offering IB classes can be expensive and time-consuming, and the research base on IB's efficacy in the United States at this point is thin. Still, more and more schools seem to be arriving at the conclusion of Kathleen Johnson, South St. Paul Junior High School's head of school: "This is probably the best K-12 education you can get."

interest-based bargaining

A departure from traditional collective bargaining, interest-based bargaining (IBB) focuses on the negotiating parties' interests (for example, those of teachers' unions and school districts), which allows the parties to consider whether they share values and goals and can find creative ways to satisfy their interests.

intruder drills

Drills schools conduct to prepare students for what to do in the event of an armed or otherwise dangerous intruder entering their school. Some critics worry that the exercises may actually heighten children's fears.

Iowa Tests Of Basic Skills

General achievement tests for grades three through eight. Along with others, such as the Comprehensive Tests of Basic Skills and the Stanford Achievement Test Series, they are designed to measure how well a student has learned the basic knowledge and skills that are taught in elementary and middle schools, in areas such as reading and mathematics.

IQ

Shorthand for "intelligence quotient," which is a person's purported mental capacity. IQ tests have become increasingly controversial because critics claim they measure only a narrow band of intellectual strengths, primarily "school smarts." Others claim the tests are biased against members of some minority groups.

J

Job Corps

A federally funded program that provides job placement and training to economically disadvantaged sixteen- to twenty-four-year-olds. Job Corps is administered by the U.S. Department of Labor.

job rotation

Students work within one industry or company in a range of occupations requiring different skills. Rotation allows students to experience the variety of jobs in one field.

job shadowing

Students accompany an employee at the workplace, observing and learning about various tasks associated with an occupation.

Juvenile Justice and Delinquency Prevention Act

The federal law providing federal funding for states' juvenile justice programs. States are required to adhere to the law's core requirements on keeping detained children safe—including limiting the time they are held in adult detention facilities—in order to receive federal money.

Kentucky Education Reform Act (KERA)

KERA was passed by the Kentucky General Assembly in 1990, following a 1989 state supreme court decision declaring that the legislature had failed to meet its (state) constitutional duty to create an "efficient" school system. It enacted new curriculum, governance, finance, and technology initiatives.

KERA established the nation's first statewide system of testing and accountability to measure progress by individual schools toward improving student learning, but the system was revamped in 1998 after complaints that the first version had yielded unreliable results and provided no data comparable with national norms.

KIPP schools

KIPP is short for "Knowledge Is Power Program." A network of college-preparatory public charter schools, KIPP schools focus on students in underserved communities and put a strong emphasis on achievement. KIPP officials say more than 80 percent of their graduates have gone on to college. (See *charter schools.*)

(Lawrence) Kohlberg

Lawrence Kohlberg (1927–1987) was an influential psychologist who studied moral development, with a particular interest in children's moral reasoning. Kohlberg posited six constructive stages of moral development. According to Kohlberg, young children view moral decisions from Stage One, which is focused on obedience and punishment. More sophisticated children move to Stage Two where they realize that different people may have different moral views. The stages grow increasingly complex. Only some people attain the highest level—Stage Six—which focuses on defining principles that foster justice.

Labeling Theory

Labeling Theory is a broad theory of social behavior that describes how attaching labels to a person (such as *deviant, disabled, high-risk,* and the like) can shape both a person's self-perception and the expectations or behavior of others toward the labeled person in ways that reinforce the label.

language-minority student

A student who comes from a home where a language other than English is spoken. According to the U.S. Census Bureau's American Community Survey, in 2006, nearly one person in five (or almost 55 million U.S. residents age five and older) spoke a language other than English at home.

learning disabilities

The term encompasses a wide variety of difficulties with learning; the criteria for it vary from state to state. In general, a learning disability describes a discrepancy between a child's intelligence and academic achievement. Some children have learning disabilities only in specific areas, such as reading or math.

learning management system (LMS)

Software designed to help with instructor-led e-learning. Sometimes a learning management system is referred to as a learning content management system (LCMS).

learning modalities

"Learning modalities" refers to the styles learners use to concentrate on, process, and retain information. The most common categories are visual (by sight), auditory (by hearing), and motor or kinesthetic (by doing things).

least restrictive environment (LRE)

The federal Individuals with Disabilities Education Act mandates that a child with disabilities be educated in the regular classroom or least restrictive environment "unless he cannot achieve satisfactorily even with the use of supplementary aides and services." The language is designed to dissuade schools from segregating children with disabilities from other students. (See *Individuals with Disabilities Education Act.*)

lesson study

A practice that involves teachers' developing and pilot-testing lessons to meet particular needs. As they discuss and analyze lessons, teachers learn more about their own craft, observers say. Following visits to Japan where the practice was used, a handful of U.S. researchers introduced lesson study to educators in the United States in the 1990s.

limited-English-proficient (LEP) students

Students enrolled in U.S. schools who speak a language other than English and haven't yet mastered English. They are also known as English-language learners. The group includes both immigrants and children born in the United States. Each state has a different way of ascertaining whether a child is limited-English-proficient. Usually such students receive bilingual education or English-as-a-second-language services. (See also *ESL, English-language learners,* and *bilingual education.*)

local education agency (LEA)

The federal government's term for a local school district. State education agencies (SEAs) are state departments of education.

local education funds (LEFs)

Community-based advocacy organizations that work to engage the public in the mission of public schools. They are independent of the public schools but traditionally work with them. The Public Education Network (PEN) is a national nonprofit organization that works with and helps launch LEFs.

lockdown

Security measure taken when there is a threat to a school. Generally, school doors are locked and students must stay in their classrooms during a lockdown. Many schools now conduct lockdown drills so students and teachers can practice what to do in the event of an emergency. (See also *intruder drills.*)

looping

A practice in which teachers work with the same group of students for more than one year. Proponents say looping—which is also called teacher-student progression and multiyear grouping—helps build stronger relationships between students and teachers and cuts down on the time needed for back-to-school reviews at the start of the school year.

"Looping" Catches On as a Way to Build Strong Ties

By Linda Jacobson, Naples, Fla.
Education Week: *October 15, 1997*

Atop the dark-green cabinets in Pat Sanford's classroom sit large, rectangular boxes labeled "sea life," "farms," and "dinosaurs." But the 2nd grade teacher at the Manatee Education Center hardly ever pulls them down to hunt for reliable old lessons that were a hit with last year's class. That's because last year's class is also this year's class—an arrangement that has forced Ms. Sanford to look continually for fresh and creative teaching materials. At least, she's got plenty of company.

All of the teachers at Manatee, a pre-K through 8th grade campus here on the edge of the Everglades, stay with their students for more than one year—an educational practice called **looping**.

magnet school

A school that places special emphasis on academic achievement or on a particular field such as science, designed to attract students from elsewhere in the school district.

mainstreaming

The practice of educating students with disabilities in regular classrooms, to the maximum extent possible. Today, advocates and educators generally call the process *inclusion* rather than mainstreaming. (See *inclusion.*)

(Horace) Mann

The renowned nineteenth-century education reformer who became Massachusetts' first education secretary in 1837. Horace Mann (1796–1859) advocated for longer school years and the instruction of students of different learning abilities in different classrooms, among other changes. He enacted reforms in Massachusetts that influenced other states. Mann is often referred to as the father of American public education.

> Hence it is, that the establishment of a republican government, without well-appointed and efficient means for the universal education of the people, is the most rash and fool-hardy experiment ever tried by man.
>
> *Horace Mann, writing in Report No. 12 of the Massachusetts School Board (1848)*

master teachers

Experienced teachers who often work with newer teachers to help them become more effective in the classroom. Master teachers also may support all teachers in improving their practice and creating ongoing professional development experiences. (See *mentoring*.)

Teacher Re-Creation

By Jeff Archer, Phoenix
Education Week: *January 10, 2001*

Debbie Ong has never been satisfied just to coast along in her job. In the 10 years she's worked as an educator, Ong has volunteered to help write her district's mathematics curriculum, earned a master's degree in elementary education from Northern Arizona University, and spent weekends learning new ways to teach fractions and geometry through a program underwritten by the National Science Foundation. The 32-year-old Ong is a **"master teacher,"** as distinguished from the "mentor teachers" and "associate teachers" in her building. Recognized by administrators and fellow teachers as an exceptionally competent educator, she puts in extra hours trying to get her skills to rub off on others by observing them, coaching them, and planning their professional growth. In return, she receives an extra $7,000 a year on top of her base pay.

mastery learning

At its most basic level, mastery learning presumes that all children can learn, given the right amount of time and instruction. Under a mastery-learning approach, children are taught a specific skill or subject in small chunks, and are tested or assessed to see if they have mastered that skill. They are retaught the skill if they have not mastered it, using a different instructional method, and then are retested. It is a cycle that can be repeated until mastery is achieved. Mastery learning may vary in implementation from school to school. Mastery learning is associated with outcomes-based education.

McKinney-Vento Homeless Assistance Act

The McKinney-Vento Homeless Assistance Act, a provision of

the No Child Left Behind Act of 2001, requires that each state ensure homeless or migrant children have access to public education equal to that of children with permanent addresses.

media literacy

An area of study focused on developing critical skills to evaluate media. Curriculum in this area is designed to help students—as early as preschool—become media-savvy and able to evaluate the messages they get from the news, entertainment, and advertising industries.

mentoring

Generally refers to an arrangement or school program whereby an experienced teacher monitors the work of a newer teacher and provides feedback and support. Mentoring is often seen as crucial to new teachers' development and job satisfaction—and thus to the stability of the teaching force. The term can also refer to guidance and support given to a student by an adult or older student. (See also *master teachers.*)

merit pay

See *performance pay.*

migrant education

Education programs established mainly to meet the needs of children of farm laborers. These children often face great challenges, including poverty and poor access to health care, as well as having to readjust to one school after another because their families move frequently. The federal government's migrant program was created in 1966 as an amendment to the Elementary and Secondary Education Act of 1965.

mixed methods research

Studies that blend different research strategies. Such a practice could include both quantitative and qualitative approaches to research. While many observers like the dual approach, some have raised questions about the cost and efficiency of mixed method research in some cases.

Modern Red Schoolhouse

A K–12 design founded in 1992 by the Hudson Institute, a think tank based in Washington. The program is now housed at the Modern Red Schoolhouse Institute in Nashville, Tennessee.

Montessori

Education method developed by Maria Montessori, an Italian physician. Montessori (1870–1952) taught that teachers should provide a "prepared environment" that entices children to explore, but that children should progress at their own pace, that it is important for them to develop a love of learning, and that they should be allowed to pursue their own interests. The teacher's role is to follow the children, observe them, and give them opportunities to develop their strengths. In a typical Montessori school, preschool and elementary-age children are organized into three mixed-age groups: three- to six-year-olds, six- to nine-year-olds, and nine- to twelve -year-olds.

motor skills

Motor skills are actions involving movement. A child with motor skill impairments has trouble moving in some way. Motor skills are generally broken into two categories: *fine motor skills* can be defined as small muscle movements that occur in the fingers, in coordination with the eyes. Fine motor skills include writing, holding small objects, and fastening buttons. *Gross motor skills* involve large muscles and affect activities such as kicking, walking, and sitting upright. Students may receive special services in school to improve either type of motor skills, or both.

multicultural education

An educational philosophy and curriculum that looks beyond the Western European tradition. Some multicultural education models highlight subjects from diverse cultural, ethnic, racial, and gender perspectives. Others represent an immersion in one culture, ethnicity, or race.

multimedia

Software that combines text, sound, video, animation, and graphics into a single presentation. The multimedia format is frequently used in edutainment software. An example of multimedia would be an electronic encyclopedia in CD-ROM format. (See also *edutainment.*)

multiple intelligences

Theory introduced by psychologist Howard Gardner in 1983. Gardner initially asserted that people are endowed with seven separate, equally valid, forms of intelligence. (Later, he added an eighth category.) Under the multiple intelligences principle, athletes and dancers, for example, might be particularly adept at exploiting "bodily-kinesthetic" intelligence, while lawyers, public speakers, and writers might demonstrate

the traits of "linguistic" intelligence. The challenge for educators, Gardner argued, is to figure out how to capitalize on those intelligences in the classroom.

Eight Forms of Intelligence

Linguistic	Spatial
Logical-mathematical	Interpersonal
Musical	Intrapersonal
Bodily-kinesthetic	Naturalist

n-size

The number of children who must belong to a subset—or subgroup—of students in order for the group's test scores to be reported separately in calculations of a school's adequate yearly progress (AYP) under the No Child Left Behind Act (NCLB). NCLB requires schools to achieve AYP with their overall student enrollment, as well as in certain subgroups: students with disabilities, students with limited English proficiency, economically disadvantaged students, white students, African American students, and Hispanic students. But the law allows individual states to determine the minimum number of students—or n-size—required for schools to report subgroup test scores. If schools do not meet their state's n-size, they do not have to break out scores by subgroup. N-sizes vary from state to state, and some states have been criticized for setting high n-sizes, making it less likely that schools would calculate AYP numbers for population subgroups.

National Assessment of Educational Progress (NAEP)

The National Assessment of Educational Progress, or NAEP, is frequently referred to as "the nation's report card." NAEP is a national testing program administered by the National Center for Education Statistics (NCES) of the U.S. Department of Education. Since 1969,

NAEP tests have been conducted periodically in reading, math, science, writing, history, and geography. The NAEP main assessment allows for regional and state-by-state comparisons of the educational attainment of fourth-, eighth-, and twelfth-grade students.

National Assessment Governing Board (NAGB)

The board that sets policy for the federally sponsored testing program known as the National Assessment of Educational Progress, or NAEP. NAGB is a bipartisan group whose twenty-six members include governors, state legislators, local and state school officials, educators, business representatives, and members of the general public. Congress created NAGB in 1988.

National College Access Network (NCAN)

See *college access programs*.

National College Advising Corps

See *college access programs*.

National Council for Accreditation of Teacher Education (NCATE)

The body that accredits more than half the nation's twelve hundred teacher-preparation programs.

National Education Association (NEA)

The nation's largest teachers' union, with 3.2 million members in 2008. The NEA is considered the most powerful teachers' union in the United States and is a frequent target of both praise and criticism from politicians on the national stage. NEA leaders have been vocal critics of the No Child Left Behind Act in recent years and have called on Congress to fully fund mandates within the law.

National Education Longitudinal Study

The U.S. Department of Education's large-scale observational study of high school and beyond. Students in the 1988 NELS were surveyed on numerous topics, including their experiences in school, the role of education in their parents' and peers' lives, characteristics of their neighborhoods, educational resources and support available to them, and their career aspirations. Officials also surveyed students' teachers, parents, and school administrators to round out the picture. Follow-up surveys with samples of students were conducted in 1990, 1992, 1994, and 2000 to gauge trends in student learning, attitudes, and behavior.

Similarly, the Education Longitudinal Study of 2002 is tracking a nationally representative group of high school students through surveys in 2002, 2004, 2006, 2010, and 2012.

National Educational Technology Standards for Students

Educational technology standards drafted by the International Society for Technology in Education. The updated standards released in 2007 are used in every state in the United States and in other countries; they emphasize skills and expertise in using digital media and new technologies.

netbooks

A newly defined class of computers that generally are small, ultralight, and energy efficient, with rugged plastic bodies, compact keyboards, and built-in antennae that can tap into wireless links to the Web. Businesses are marketing netbooks to schools as less expensive alternatives to traditional laptop computers.

new math

The term originally referred to brief, dramatic changes in the way math was taught in the U.S. in the 1960s. The teaching of "new math" concepts varied widely, but it essentially embodied more abstract ways of thinking about mathematics. New math eventually faded out and came to be viewed by the public as a failed curriculum-reform effort. In recent years, observers have labeled certain newer reforms "new, new math." With impetus from math standards issued by the National Council of Teachers of Mathematics in 1989, some schools are moving to math curricula with a greater emphasis on problem solving. Critics charge that this shift comes at the expense of teaching basic skills.

(The) New Teacher Project

Since spinning off from Teach For America in 1997, The New Teacher Project (TNTP), a nonprofit organization led mostly by former teachers, has partnered with more than two hundred districts, including Atlanta, Chicago, the District of Columbia, and New York City. TNTP works with districts and states to recruit, select, hire, and train new teachers. Experts attribute the organization's success to its holistic approach; besides recruiting and training, it helps districts streamline and update antiquated hiring practices that, the project's officials say, keep new teachers away. It also offers certification programs in content areas in some states.

No Child Left Behind Act

The No Child Left Behind (NCLB) Act of 2001, signed into law by President Bush on January 8, 2002, is a reauthorization of the Elementary and Secondary Education Act, the central federal law in precollegiate education. The ESEA, first enacted in 1965 and reauthorized a total of eight times as of 2008, includes Title I, the federal government's flagship aid program for disadvantaged students. The act's Title III is the conduit for most federal funding for English-language-learner programs.

As the newest incarnation of the ESEA, the No Child Left Behind Act has expanded the federal role in education and become a focal point of education policy. Coming at a time of wide public concern about the state of education, the legislation sets in place requirements that reach into virtually every public school in America. It takes particular aim at improving the educational lot of disadvantaged students. NCLB centers on numerous measures designed to improve achievement and accountability in schools, including ensuring that schools are making what is termed "adequate yearly progress" in student achievement and employing teachers deemed to be "highly qualified." NCLB mandates that states test students in reading and mathematics in Grades 3–8 and once in high school, ranking them as either advanced, proficient, basic, or below basic. Under the law, all students must be proficient in those subjects by the 2013–14 school year. (See also *accountability, Elementary and Secondary Education Act, highly qualified teacher,* and *Title I.*)

Excerpt from statement by President George W. Bush on January 8, 2002, as he signed the bill into law (during a ceremony at Hamilton High School in Hamilton, Ohio: "The fundamental principle of this bill is that every child can learn, we expect every child to learn, and you must show us whether or not every child is learning."

nonverbal learning disorder (NLD)

A neurophysiologic disorder that impairs a person's ability to take in nonverbal information. Children with NLDs generally fail to understand social cues, meaning they have trouble interpreting facial expressions and body language, which can lead to their social isolation and misunderstanding of many common situations. Their poor visual-spatial abilities may also make it hard for them to learn math concepts. In addition, while children with an NLD may have good vocabularies, they may have trouble with reading comprehension and oral and written comprehension. An NLD can affect an individual's ability to succeed in both academic and nonacademic areas.

norm-referenced test

A standardized test designed primarily to compare the performance of students with that of their peers nationally. Such tests do not generally measure how students perform in relation to a state's own academic standards. (See also *criterion-referenced test.*)

(Robert) Noyce Teacher Scholarships

The Robert Noyce Teacher Scholarship program seeks to encourage talented science, technology, engineering, and mathematics majors and professionals to become K–12 mathematics and science teachers. The program gives funding to colleges and universities to support scholarships, stipends, and programs for students who commit to teaching in high-need K–12 school districts.

numeracy

The ability to think mathematically and to master mathematical concepts such as addition, subtraction, simple multiplication and division, and money counting.

occupational therapy (OT)

Occupational therapy is a specialized area of physical treatment designed to help people perform daily tasks of living. In the case of children, occupational therapy (OT) is aimed at helping them learn and may be required as part of a child's individualized education program (IEP) under the Individuals with Disabilities Education Act. OTs' practices may resemble play, but they can be geared to helping students overcome delays or learning troubles. (See also *Individuals with Disabilities Education Act* and *individualized education program*.)

Office for Civil Rights (OCR)

The U.S. Department of Education's Office for Civil Rights (OCR) is charged with investigating discrimination complaints involving schools and students.

Office of Special Education Programs (OSEP)

The Office of Special Education Programs (OSEP) in the U.S. Department of Education focuses on improving outcomes for children from birth through age twenty-one. OSEP authorizes formula grants to states and oversees discretionary grant programs in special education, as well.

Office of Special Education and Rehabilitative Services (OSERS)

The Office of Special Education and Rehabilitative Services (OSERS) in the U.S. Department of Education emphasizes three priorities: special education, vocational rehabilitation, and research. OSERS funds initiatives for children and adults with disabilities.

One Laptop Per Child Foundation

A nonprofit foundation that has enlisted corporations and governments to provide computers to children in developing countries, with the ultimate goal of eliminating poverty.

open classroom

A school-design model of the 1970s that has since faded from popularity. The concept often translated into "schools without walls." Open classrooms were designed to be large learning spaces where multiple teachers would work with students of various skills levels. Most schools eventually abandoned the literal open classroom and installed walls for smaller, individual classes. The open classroom concept—emphasizing collaboration—continues to thrive in some schools, however.

open educational resources

Free, publicly funded education materials made available via the Internet. The idea behind open educational resources (OER) is that releasing educational materials into the open arena gives all students— regardless of income level or geographic location—access to valuable curricula, while it helps educators continually improve and update learning materials. One example of an OER is FreeReading, an open instructional program designed to help teach early literacy through a forty-week scope and sequence of concepts and activities. (See *open source*.)

open enrollment

Open enrollment is a policy allowing students to transfer in and out of schools as long as space is available.

open source

In education, the term refers to a movement to provide software and other educational materials to schools for free. (See also *open educational resources*.)

oppositional defiant disorder (ODD)

The American Academy of Child & Adolescent Psychiatry defines children with ODD as manifesting "an ongoing pattern of uncooperative, defiant, and hostile behavior toward authority figures that seriously interferes with the youngster's day-to-day functioning."

outcomes-based education (OBE)

A school reform movement in the 1990s that focused on students' ability to show they have learned certain materials. OBE is the theory that students learn better when expectations for student achievement are measured by changes in knowledge, skills, and attitudes rather than by grades. Some states pursued OBE standards, but conservatives lashed out at OBE, charging that it focused on social values—often liberal social values—instead of academic achievement.

Software Solution Saves Dollars

By Andrew Trotter
Education Week: *September 29, 2004*

A growing number of cost-conscious school districts are finding budget relief in low-cost computer software known as **"open source"** that can do everything from manage school Web sites to equip classrooms for learning. Administrators cite open-source-related savings of hundreds of dollars per new computer, plus benefits such as reduced exposure to computer viruses and to copyright violations. Open source refers to software distributed with a proviso that gives anyone the right to dissect, modify, and redistribute or even resell it, on the condition that the people receiving it have the same right. The software typically is developed through online collaborations between programmers and users that can reach across the world. The software is usually created for the open-source operating system Linux, but can also be designed to run on Microsoft Windows and Apple Macintosh operating systems.

P

P-16/P-20 councils or initiatives

A council or effort that seeks to advise state governments and shape policy on how to integrate a student's education beginning in preschool (as early as three years old) through a four-year college degree and even graduate school. Many states are trying to connect education along the P-16/P-20 spectrum to better prepare students for further study, work, and citizenship.

PTA

The Parent Teacher Association (PTA) calls itself the largest volunteer child advocacy association in the United States. A national nonprofit organization with chapters at the state and local school level across the country, the PTA's goal is "a quality education and nurturing environment for every child."

paraprofessionals

Teachers' aides. Under the No Child Left Behind Act, paraprofessionals can take one of three routes to attain NCLB's highly qualified status: acquire an associate's degree, take at least two years' worth of college courses, or pass a test that measures knowledge and ability to assist teachers in teaching math, reading, and writing.

Parental Information and Resource Centers (PIRCs)

In most cases, Parental Information and Resource Centers, or PIRCs, are private, nonprofit organizations that receive federal money under the No Child Left Behind Act to implement successful parental involvement policies and practices.

parochial school

A private school operated by a religious organization, often a church. Parochial schools combine theological and academic education.

pedagogy

The art or science of teaching. Some people refer also to a "signature pedagogy," or a systematic, shared set of practices that distinguishes the preparation programs in a given profession. Observers often debate the need for pedagogy training for new teachers relative to grounding them deeply in the subject matter they plan to teach.

peer coaching

When two or more teachers work together in a collaborative and confidential fashion to improve each other's practice.

peer review

When teachers evaluate other teachers' performance. Typically, peer review partners an inexperienced teacher with a more senior educator. The two can share ideas and observe each other's classrooms; ultimately, the senior teacher reviews the other's performance.

peer tutoring

Also called "peer-assisted learning." When students help instruct other students. More than thirty years' worth of studies of elementary-level peer-tutoring programs suggests that both the tutor and the student being tutored learn better when they work with each other than they do in regular teacher-led classrooms.

Pell grants

A form of financial aid for college students from lower-income families. Pell grants are awarded by the federal government and do not have to be repaid.

performance-based assessment

Requires students to perform hands-on tasks, such as writing an essay or conducting a science experiment. Such assessments are becoming increasingly common as alternatives to multiple-choice, machine-scored tests. Also known as "authentic assessment."

performance pay

Any of a number of plans to pay teachers on the basis of their demonstrated competence in teaching, rather than on their number of years in the profession. The pay plans are controversial because many believe it is difficult to objectively identify and quantify good teaching. Also known as "merit pay." One of the nation's best-known performance pay plans is Denver's ProComp, or the Professional Compensation Plan for teachers, as it is formally known. ProComp was mandated by Denver voters in 2004.

States Giving Performance Pay by Doling Out Bonuses

Alaska, Florida, and Texas latest to tie cash to student test scores.

By Michele McNeil
Education Week: *September 6, 2006*

In Texas this school year, teachers have money riding on their students' achievement. Up to $10,000, in fact, under a new program designed to reward high-performing teachers in high-poverty districts, and encourage other teachers to do better. Though many states have debated changing the way teachers are paid, Texas is one of just three that have succeeded in linking compensation for individual teachers with student achievement. At the end of this school year, teachers in about 1,000 Texas schools will be eligible for cash bonuses, which will likely range from $3,000 to $10,000, for boosting student performance.

(Carl D.) Perkins Career and Technical Education and Improvement Act

The federal vocational education law. The law emphasizes the academic achievement of students in career and technical education and seeks to improve connections between secondary and postsecondary education.

persistently dangerous schools

A term from the No Child Left Behind Act. Under NCLB, students may receive help transferring out of schools that are deemed "persistently dangerous." This has proved tricky, however, as each state sets its own standards for the label. Critics say the term is so pejorative that educators hesitate to apply it to most schools.

pervasive developmental disorder—not otherwise specified (PDD-NOS)

A disorder on the autism spectrum; also referred to as "atypical personality development," "atypical PDD," or "atypical autism." The Yale Child Study Center writes that PDD-NOS encompasses "cases where there is marked impairment of social interaction, communication, and/or stereotyped behavior patterns or interest, but when full features for autism or another explicitly defined PDD are not met."

Phi Delta Kappa

A professional membership association for educators. The organization advocates for public schools and maintains individual member chapters in the United States, Canada, Europe, and Asia. Phi Delta Kappa also publishes the education journal *Phi Delta Kappan,* and sponsors the annual Phi Delta Kappa/Gallup Poll of the Public's Attitudes Toward the Public Schools.

Phonological Awareness Literacy Screening tests (PALS)

The PALS system, developed by researchers at the University of Virginia, has served as the early-literacy assessment in Virginia since 1997. It is used by schools and districts in more than forty other states as well.

phonemic awareness

The recognition that sounds make up language. The International Reading Association describes phonemic awareness as "the ability to segment and manipulate the sounds of oral language." Phonemic awareness is one of the five elements of instruction identified by the National Reading Panel as essential for helping students to become proficient readers. (The others are phonics, fluency, vocabulary, and comprehension.)

phonics

An instructional strategy used to teach letter-sound relationships to beginning readers by having them "sound out" words letter by letter. Phonics is one of the five essential elements of instruction identified by the National Reading Panel as essential for helping students to become proficient readers. (The others are fluency, phonemic awareness, vocabulary, and comprehension.)

(Jean) Piaget

A leading educational thinker of the early twentieth century. Jean Piaget (1896–1980) was a Swiss psychologist who identified four stages that characterize children's learning abilities from birth onward.

"The principle goal of education is to create men who are capable of doing new things, not simply of repeating what other generations have done—men who are creative, inventive and discoverers."

Jean Piaget, 1954, from the book,
The Construction of Reality in the Child

Piaget's Stages of Cognitive Development

The Sensorimotor Stage: Lasts approximately from birth to age two and is centered about the infant trying to understand the world through sensory input.

The Preoperational Stage: From ages two to six. Language development and understanding symbols are key components of this stage.

The Concrete Operational Stage: From ages seven to about eleven . In this stage, children begin to think logically about concrete events. They still have trouble understanding abstract issues.

The Formal Operational Stage: From age twelve into adulthood. During this stage, people learn how to think abstractly and to employ deductive reasoning.

Plyler v. *Doe*

The 1982 U.S. Supreme Court decision in which the court ruled that children are entitled to receive a free public K–12 education regardless of their immigration status. The court struck down a Texas statute that withheld from local school districts any state funds that went for the education of any children not "legally admitted" into the United States, and authorized districts to bar their enrollment, as a violation of the 14th Amendment's equal-protection clause.

popcorn reading

Colloquial term for a classroom practice where students "pop in" to read during a teacher-led reading exercise. Unlike round-robin reading, in which students in a circle or row take turns reading in order, popcorn reading is more open in that students can participate when they feel ready and in whatever order they choose.

Working Smarter by Working Together

By Vaishali Honawar
Lincolnshire, Ill.
Education Week: *April 2, 2008*

Adlai E. Stevenson High School was one of the first in the nation to embrace what are known as **professional learning communities.** The Illinois school's focus on teacher teamwork has catapulted it from an ordinary good school to an extraordinary one, advocates say. Among its many accolades, it has been a U.S. Department of Education Blue Ribbon school for four years—one of only three nationwide to achieve that honor. Moreover, as many as 96 percent of Stevenson's students go on to college. So well known are the learning communities here that each year, 3,000 people visit the school's sprawling campus 30 miles northwest of Chicago to experience firsthand how its teacher-collaboration model works. In a professional learning community, each teacher has access to the ideas, materials, strategies, and talents of the entire team. At Stevenson, teachers meet in course-specific, and sometimes interdisciplinary, teams each week to discuss strategies for improvement; craft common assessments, the results of which are analyzed to improve instruction; and brainstorm lesson plans. Instead of the isolation of their classrooms, they spend their time between classes and before and after school in open office areas where their desks abut those of their course peers. The arrangement ensures that the give-and-take between teacher teams is almost constant.

portfolio

A systematic and organized collection of a student's work throughout a course or class year. It measures the student's knowledge and skills and often includes some form of self-reflection by the student.

Praxis

A widely used series of tests for prospective teachers. Praxis I tests measure basic academic skills; Praxis II tests measure general and subject-specific knowledge and teaching skills. Praxis III assessments measure classroom performance of beginning teachers. The tests were created by the Educational Testing Service (ETS).

prekindergarten

See *universal preschool.*

private school

An independent school run by an individual or agency other than the state or district. It is usually supported by private funds and is not controlled by publicly elected or appointed officials. (See *independent school.*)

privatization

Transfer of the management of public schools to private or for-profit education organizations. Privatization emphasizes typical business-oriented concepts such as customer satisfaction and managerial autonomy in running schools.

ProComp

See *performance pay.*

professional development

Activities designed to enhance the teaching skills and professionalism of educators. High-quality professional development is considered essential to good teaching.

professional learning community (PLC)

A PLC comprises collaborative teams whose members, usually teachers, work interdependently to improve learning for all students.

Program for International Student Assessment (PISA)

Standardized international science and mathematics exams in which the achievement of students from various nations is compared. The test measures the performance of fifteen-year-old students, regardless of grade level, examining the skills they pick up both in the classroom and outside school, as well as their ability to apply that knowledge to a variety of situations. Unlike some national and international tests, PISA takes into account learning that may occur outside formal academic settings. Science literacy is defined by the Organization for Economic Cooperation and Development, or OECD, which oversees PISA. Thirty industrialized countries took part in the program's 2006 science exams, and U.S. students ranked lower, on average, than their counterparts in sixteen other countries.

Progress in International Reading Literacy Study (PIRLS)

An exam that gauges literacy among fourth graders on a five-year cycle; fifty countries participated in 2006. The test, administered by the International Association for the Evaluation of Educational Achievement, based in Amsterdam, was first given in 2001.

Progressive education

A school of thought traditionally associated with more active learning, cooperative planning by teachers and students, a greater recognition of individual differences, attempts to relate learning to "real life," and efforts to broaden a school's mission to address health, vocational, social, and community issues. That said, there is great variety within the progressive education field. Progressive education is often divided into three main strands: child-centered progressives, social progressives, and administrative progressives. The most famous voice to come out of the progressive movement in education was the philosopher and educator John Dewey. (See *(John) Dewey.*)

project-based learning
An approach to learning targeted skills and knowledge that emphasizes answering essential questions and solving real-world problems, often with students working in teams.

prompt
Directions, a scenario, a question, or a combination of those that set out a writing task for a student, with the type of prompt varying with the type of writing—descriptive, persuasive, or creative, for example—being taught.

public engagement
The involvement of parents, community members, and taxpayers in efforts to improve schools and learning.

pull-out
Removing a child or children from regular classroom settings for either remedial or enrichment coursework. (See *enrichment.*)

quasi-experimental study

A study that is similar to a true experiment except for the fact that subjects are not randomly assigned to the comparison groups. For example, a study of the effectiveness of the Reading First federal literacy program relied on a "regression discontinuity" design, in which participants were assigned to program or comparison groups solely on the basis of a cutoff score on a preprogram measure. (See *Reading First.*)

R

randomized controlled trial (RCT)

An experiment in which investigators randomly assign subjects or units such as classrooms or schools to either an intervention group or a control group.

Reading First

A federal program first rolled out in 2002 to improve reading instruction in the nation's struggling schools. While widely viewed as beneficial for improving reading instruction in elementary schools with large proportions of disadvantaged children, Reading First was the focus of several federal investigations and congressional hearings from 2005 to 2007 and was in danger of being defunded for fiscal 2009.

reading fluency

The ability to read text passages aloud accurately and smoothly at an appropriate pace. Students who read aloud easily are more likely to understand what they are reading, both silently and orally, according to a study of fourth graders who took the 2002 National Assessment of Educational Progress (NAEP) in reading. Fluency is one of the five essential elements of instruction identified by the National Reading Panel as essential for helping students to become proficient readers. (The others are phonics, phonemic awareness, vocabulary, and comprehension.) (See *phonemic awareness* and *phonics*.)

Reading Recovery

An intensive one-to-one tutoring program. In 2007, federal researchers found positive effects or potentially positive effects for Reading Recovery across all four of the domains in their review—alphabetics, fluency, comprehension, and general reading achievement. Previously, the program had drawn criticism from prominent researchers and federal officials who claimed it was not scientifically based or cost-effective.

ReadWriteThink

An International Reading Association collaboration with the National Council of Teachers of English. ReadWriteThink integrates Internet content into lesson plans designed to promote critical literacy. (See *critical literacy*.)

reauthorization

The renewal and updating of federal laws by the U.S. Congress. All federal education laws—including the No Child Left Behind Act and Individuals with Disabilities Education Act—must be periodically reviewed by Congress and then reauthorized, often with significant changes. Reauthorized bills must be signed by the president to enact their new provisions.

reconstitution

When a state or district replaces some or all of a troubled school's staff members and essentially relaunches the school in hopes of eradicating failing practices and policies. Reconstitution is often wrenching and divisive in that it goes to the heart of a school's culture. While proponents believe the threat of reconstitution can motivate school improvement, critics charge that it is demoralizing and disruptive and fails to address underlying equity issues.

redistricting

The process of redefining the boundary of an area that is unified for some purpose. This includes but is not limited to the consolidation or breakup of school districts.

reform network

An association of educators, schools, or districts joined together to provide mutual support as they work on common plans for improving education. Popular reform networks include Theodore Sizer's Coalition of Essential Schools and James Comer's School Development Program. (See *Comer schools*.)

Reggio Emilia Approach

The preschools of Reggio Emilia, Italy—and the particular educational philosophy at work there—have long fascinated early-childhood educators in the United States. The Reggio Emilia approach views the teacher as one who explores, learns, and creates along with the child, and it treats the environment as the "third teacher," which means classrooms are made into beautiful spaces by using natural light, plants, large windows, and the children's own artwork.

remedial education, remediation

Instruction that seeks to bring students deficient in basic skills up to standard levels in essential subjects such as writing, reading, and math.

report cards

The periodic evaluations of a student's academic progress, usually sent home to parents. Separately, some districts use so-called school report cards to inform the public about the performance of individual schools by means of student test scores and other measures.

response to intervention (RTI)

An educational process of providing targeted, scientifically validated instruction to students as soon as testing identifies a youngster's areas of weakness. Student progress is consistently monitored so teachers can tailor their lessons to a student's needs. The RTI process is also used in behavior management programs in schools.

"Response to Intervention" Sparks Interest, Questions

Critics say approach depends on too many complex factors.

By Christina A. Samuels
Education Week: *January 23, 2008*

In most **RTI** programs, students are given a basic screening early in the school year, to spot any potential educational deficits. Those who may have difficulties are given additional tests, to allow school-based teams to zero in on the problems and craft an approach to addressing them. Students are then given intensive education in a "multi-tiered" system of service delivery. The small numbers of students who do not respond well to any interventions are considered to be at the top of the tiers, and are more carefully evaluated for possible referral to special education services. The promise is that general education teachers will be able to accurately identify the problems that students are having, and nip those in the bud before they lead to entrenched difficulties, or referral to special education.

retention

The process of holding low-achieving students back for a year in school. This is different from **"teacher retention,"** which refers to efforts to keep teachers in the profession.

Ritalin

The most widely used drug to treat attention deficit hyperactivity disorder, a condition characterized by an inability to concentrate affecting between 3 and 10 percent of U.S. school-age children. Ritalin, the trade name for the drug methylphenidate, is said to help filter out unwanted stimuli in the brain. Other stimulant drugs used to treat ADD and AD/HD include Concerta (also methylphenidate), amphetamines (Adderall), dexmethylphenidate (Focalin), and dextroamphetamine (Dexedrine). By comparison, Strattera, also known by its generic name atomoxetine, is a nonstimulant drug approved for treatment of ADD and AD/HD. (See also *Attention Deficit / Hyperactivity Disorder.*)

rubric

An assessment tool that offers objective standards for gauging subjective work, such as student essays. Critics question whether these standards can effectively gauge such skills as a child's ability to write well.

S

Safe and Drug-Free Schools and Communities program

Federal program that funds efforts to address issues ranging from reducing student fights to stopping gun violence.

safe harbor provisions

Allowances in the No Child Left Behind Act designed to give a second chance to schools that don't make adequate yearly progress (AYP) initially. The provisions allow schools credit for making adequate progress as long as more students maintained or moved up to proficiency in the current school year than in the preceding one. (See *No Child Left Behind Act.*)

SAT

The SAT is a standardized test, usually taken to predict a student's readiness for college. The SAT I: Reasoning Test, updated in 2005, is a test of written, verbal, and mathematical reasoning ability. The SAT II: Subject Tests, formerly known as Achievement Tests, are tests of current ability and knowledge in high school subject areas such as English and biology.

Sample SAT-style Questions

Choose the word or set of words that, when inserted into the sentence, best fits the meaning of the sentence as a whole.

Although the opposing factions were not able to achieve _____, they left the jury room in _____.

A. ✦ unity . . . discord

B. ✦ agreement . . . anger

C. ✦ leniency . . . silence

D. ✦ consensus . . . amity

E. ✦ deliberations . . . disarray

In a drawer are 7 pairs of white socks, 9 pairs of black socks, and 6 pairs of brown socks. Getting dressed in a hurry, Josh pulls out a pair at a time and tosses them on the floor if they are not the color he wants. Looking for a brown pair, Josh pulls out and discards a white pair, a black pair, a black pair, and a white pair. What is the probability that on his next reach into the drawer he will pull out a brown pair of socks?

A. ✦ 1/3

B. ✦ 3/11

C. ✦ 6/17

D. ✦ 7/18

E. ✦ 9/22

Answers: D *and* A

scaffolding

A metaphor used to describe the type of support that teachers (and, in some cases, peers) offer students as they are learning a new concept. Much like a physical scaffold that holds workers temporarily while they tackle a project, teacher scaffolding or support is there for individual students while they are mastering an idea; it can then be removed or reconfigured to help with other learning. The practice of scaffolding draws on developmental psychologist Lev Vygotsky's ideas on children's potential for learning and their need for help from other, more skilled individuals to learn new skills. (See *zone of proximal development.*)

SCANS Report

A massive two-year project of the U.S. Department of Labor. The Secretary's Commission on Achieving Necessary Skills (SCANS) in 1992 recommended a host of changes to make school curricula and teaching methods more relevant to the modern workplace.

school administration manager

A manager who oversees the day-to-day business aspects of running a school. With so much expected academically of principals, some schools today hire administration managers so principals can focus on teachers, students, and learning.

school-based budgeting

The practice by which individual schools are given considerable control over spending instead of having to follow district-wide funding mandates.

school choice

Any proposal that allows children to attend schools outside their local district boundaries. Choice has two basic forms, the less controversial being *voluntary public school choice.* Public school choice involves parents' opting to send their children to a public school other than their neighborhood school. This might mean choosing to send their children to a magnet school or simply to another school in their district with better test scores or other appealing features. The more controversial choice option is *private school choice,* in which advocates and parents ask the government to grant them a voucher or other support to underwrite the cost of private school tuition. Parents in failing school districts who cannot afford to send their children to private school on their own often say private choice is the only way to guarantee their children an adequate education. (See also *tuition tax credits* and *vouchers.*)

school-community links

Efforts by schools to reach out to parents, families, community leaders, and human-services professionals to improve community life and address social issues that impede learning. Examples range from making school space available for before- and after-school programs to connecting a family to services in the community to planning better long-range coordination of services.

school-community services

Activities offered on or near school sites to benefit families and other neighborhood residents. Such activities include child care, adult education, recreation, counseling, health screening, mentoring, tutoring, conflict resolution, parent education, job training, cultural and arts programs, and drop-in centers for teenagers.

school interoperability framework (SIF)

A method of exchanging data among various school software applications. SIF specifications are based on agreements among software publishers about how their software describes data, so it can be recognized and used by any compliant software and for many different purposes.

school finance

The term refers to federal, state, and local mechanisms for funding schools. Over the years, numerous school finance lawsuits have been filed disputing either the equity of state funding systems (citing disparities among the tax bases of local schools and per-pupil spending) or the adequacy of the money a state provides to schools generally.

school reform

A generic term encompassing all kinds of efforts to improve schools. Reform efforts focus on all aspects of schooling, from how schools are governed to what curriculum is taught in the classroom.

school-to-work transition

Any of a host of programs from on-the-job training to apprenticeships to cooperative agreements between high schools and community colleges designed to prepare students not bound for college to enter the job market.

Schools and Staffing Survey (SASS)

Produced by the U.S. Department of Education's National Center on Education Statistics, SASS is the nation's most extensive survey of elementary and secondary schools and their teachers and administrators. SASS has four core components: the School Questionnaire, the Teacher Questionnaire, the Principal Questionnaire, and the School District Questionnaire, which was known as the Teacher Demand and Shortage Questionnaire until the 1999–2000 SASS administration. Surveys are sent to public, private, and Bureau of Indian Affairs tribal schools. They collect data on teacher demand and shortages, teacher and administrator characteristics, school climate, and general conditions in schools.

schools within schools

Smaller learning communities within large high schools. These communities may be built around certain curriculum themes. Starting with the idea that many U.S. high schools are too large and impersonal to serve students well, many districts in recent years have pursued the option of breaking up their large high schools into smaller schools within schools rather than following the more costly path of building new and smaller stand-alone schools. The U.S. Department of Education for many years has provided grant money for its Smaller Learning Communities Program—aid districts may use to create schools within schools.

scientifically based research

While definitions vary, the term is generally taken to refer to studies that use randomized controlled trials or other very rigorous research methods. The term is featured most prominently in the No Child Left Behind Act, which cites it more than one hundred times.

SCORM

Abbreviation for Sharable Content Object Reference Model. SCORM is a collection of standards for developing and packaging e-learning materials.

Scripps National Spelling Bee

The world's best-known student spelling competition. The bee is generally open to students who have not reached their sixteenth birthday on or before the date of the national finals and who have not passed beyond the eighth grade at the time of their school finals. Students compete in locally sponsored spelling competitions, and winners move on to the annual national finals in Washington, D.C.

Scripps National Spelling Bee Winning Words and Students

2000: demarche

George Abraham Thampy
St. Louis, Missouri

2001: succedaneum

Sean Conley
Aitkin, Minnesota

2002: prospicience

Pratyush Buddiga
Denver, Colorado

2003: pococurante

Sai R. Gunturi
Dallas, Texas

2004: autochthonous

David Scott Pilarski Tidmarsh
South Bend, Indiana

2005: appoggiatura

Anurag Kashyap
San Diego, California

Section 504 of the Rehabilitation Act of 1973

The law prohibits discrimination against people with disabilities by agencies that receive federal funding. All students covered under the Individuals with Disabilities Education Act (IDEA) also receive Section 504 protection. However, a small group of students may be eligible for accommodations under Section 504 while not being eligible for special education through IDEA because of the nature of their disabilities. Section 504 has a three-part definition to quality for services that is broader than IDEA's: A student must have (1) a physical or mental impairment that (2) substantially limits (3) one or more "major life activities." (See also *Individuals with Disabilities Education Act.*)

self-regulated strategy development (SRSD)

Initially developed for students with learning disabilities or difficulties, SRSD is a practice in which students are explicitly taught writing strategies and skills for self-regulation, including goal-setting and self-reinforcement.

sensory integration disorder or dysfunction (SID)

A neurological disorder that occurs when the brain cannot fully process information taken in through the five senses. May also be referred to as sensory processing disorder, or SPD. A child with SID may either over-respond to sensory information and find certain noises or touches, for example, unbearable; another child might underrespond and show little reaction to sensations, even painful ones. Either situation can lead to difficulties in school and everyday life.

service learning

Programs that incorporate citizenship values into education by requiring students to perform community service. In some districts, community service is a mandatory requirement for graduation.

sexual harassment

Unwelcome written or verbal comments or physical gestures or actions of a sexual nature.

In 1999, the U.S. Supreme Court ruled that schools receiving federal funds may be sued for damages for peer sexual harassment under Title IX of the Education Amendments of 1972. Schools can be held liable, the majority emphasized, only when officials show deliberate indifference to information about "severe, pervasive and objectively offensive" harassment that interferes with a student's access to an educational program or benefit. The Court issued its 5–4 decision in *Davis* v. *Monroe County Board of Education.*

Separately, in *Gebser* v. *Lago Vista Independent School District* in 1998, the Supreme Court provided school districts with general guidance on how to avoid liability under Title IX for sex harassment of students by teachers. Schools can be liable for damages, the Court said, if a school district official with authority to take corrective measures has notice of and is deliberately indifferent to an employee's misconduct.

Md. Service Learning: Classroom Link Weak?

By Michelle Galley
Education Week: *October 15, 2003*

Maryland students are mucking out horse stalls, dancing in ballets, answering telephones, and ladling soup for the homeless in order to graduate from high school. Eleven years after the legislature passed a first-of-its-kind state law requiring all public school students to complete 75 hours of **service learning**, young people are fulfilling the requirement with varying degrees of success. Proponents of service learning maintain that regardless of how routine a task may seem, young men and women are still gaining valuable skills and performing needed services in the community.

single-gender or single-sex education

Schools or classes devoted to educating only boys or girls. In 2006, the U.S. Department of Education issued final regulations that definitively state it is legal to educate boys and girls separately under certain conditions. Such programs must be related to improving the achievement of students, providing diverse educational opportunities, or meeting the needs of particular students, and they must treat boys and girls evenhandedly. Proponents of single-sex education point to research and sentiment among some educators that separating boys and girls, and teaching to what are often viewed as their different learning styles, may help students of both sexes perform better in school. (See *Title IX.*)

single salary schedule

Paying teachers based on a single salary schedule that pays men and women and elementary and secondary teachers the same. Teachers are paid according to how many years they have been teaching and how many educational credits or degrees they have accumulated.

site-based management

The shift of decision-making authority from the centralized school district office to local schools. The goal is to place more authority and accountability with individual schools with an eye toward improving student achievement.

social and emotional learning (SEL)

School-based programs that aim to teach students to manage their emotions and to practice empathy, caring, and cooperation. Such programs might include character education lessons, anti-bullying efforts, drug-abuse-prevention programs, or conflict-resolution training. Social and emotional learning programs have a small but growing presence in schools.

social networking

The use of the Internet, e-mail, and cell phone texting to build social connections. Popular commercial Web sites such as Facebook.com and MySpace.com offer students (and educators) a free, easy way to create personal Web pages and fill them with content: text diaries or blogs, digital snapshots, favorite songs, and short video clips. Social networks are formed as members link their Web pages to those of their friends and search through the vast sites to find new friends who share common interests. Beyond the sites' social aspects, students and some educators say they offer young people a valuable showcase for writing and other forms of self-expression. But social networking poses risks, too, that students will share inappropriate private information or use the Web to engage in online bullying. In response, many schools have banned use of social networking sites on campus, though often not effectively. (See *blog, cyberbullying.*)

social promotion

The practice of advancing children to the next grade in school despite their inability to meet the usual academic standards for promotion.

Socratic method

A means of teaching and learning that involves posing a series of questions framed around a central topic. The person asking the questions also must answer others' queries, and often the two sides take opposing views of the issue at hand. The method is named for Socrates, once declared the wisest man in ancient Athens.

special education

Programs designed to serve children with mental and physical disabilities. Such children are entitled to individualized education plans (IEPs) that spell out the services needed to reach their educational goals, ranging from speech therapy to math tutoring. Traditionally, special education has taken place in separate classrooms. Increasingly, the services may also be offered in regular schools and classrooms. (See *individualized education plans.*)

staff development

See *professional development.*

standards

Subject-matter benchmarks to measure students' academic achievement. Curriculum standards drive what students learn in the classroom. Most educators agree that public schools' academic standards need to be raised, but there is intense national debate over how to implement such standards—how prescriptive they should be, and whether they should be national or local, voluntary or mandated.

State Child Health Insurance Program (SCHIP)

A children's health insurance program partially financed by the federal government. SCHIP is aimed at children in families that earn too much to be eligible for Medicaid but find it hard to afford private health insurance. In 2007, about 6.6 million children and 670,000 adults were insured through SCHIP, which varies in structure and income eligibility from state to state.

Standards for Success

In 2003, this project, sponsored by the Association of American Universities and the Pew Charitable Trusts, published a document describing the knowledge and skills students would need to succeed in entry-level courses and to major in specific academic areas in the nation's leading research universities. The standards have since been licensed by the College Board, the sponsor of the SAT and Advanced Placement exams. Among other purposes, the College Board has used the standards to develop SpringBoard, a mathematics, reading, and writing program for sixth through twelfth graders designed to prepare all youngsters for college-level work, including AP courses.

Stanford Achievement Test Series

Popular standardized tests for assessing children in kindergarten through high school. The Stanford 10—the tenth edition in the series—is a multiple-choice assessment aimed at learning what students know and are able to do. The tests gauge student knowledge in mathematics and reading, and, in some cases, science and social sciences.

Stanford-Binet Intelligence Test

A standardized test used for assessing intelligence in children and young adults. The Stanford-Binet launched the modern era of testing for intelligence, or IQ. It assesses intelligence in four areas: verbal reasoning, quantitative reasoning, abstract and visual reasoning, and short-term memory. (See *IQ*.)

stereotype threat

The idea that people tend to underperform when confronted with situations that might confirm negative stereotypes about their social group. Stanford University psychologist Claude M. Steele made headlines in 1995 with a study that introduced the phrase "stereotype threat." Steele's original research involved black college students whose test performance faltered when they were told they were taking an exam that would measure intellectual ability, but the effect has since been documented in more than two hundred studies involving all sorts of situations. Scholars have found evidence of "stereotype threat" occurring, for example, among elementary school girls taking mathematics tests, elderly people given a memory test, and white men being assessed on athletic ability. Even something as subtle as asking students to indicate their race or gender on a test form can trigger the phenomenon, some of those studies have suggested.

structured English immersion

Structured English immersion is generally defined as providing limited-English-proficient children with "nearly all" of their classroom instruction in English but using curriculum and presentation that recognizes that LEP students are still learning English. (See *bilingual education* and *limited-English-proficient (LEP) students*.)

Student/Teacher Achievement Ratio Experiment (STAR)

A longitudinal research study on class-size reduction in Tennessee; the most famous experiment on the topic. The students in the project were randomly assigned to classes ranging in size from thirteen to twenty-five students in grades K–3 from 1985 to 1989. Early findings showed that students in the smaller classes—which ranged from thirteen to seventeen students—outperformed their peers on reading and mathematics tests. Later on, when the students returned to regular classes, they maintained their academic edge, staying from six to thirteen months ahead of their peers from larger classes during Grades 4, 6, and 8 in math, reading, and science. The researchers also found that poor students from inner-city schools tended to gain the most from smaller classes. Project STAR was paid for by the Tennessee legislature and involved roughly seven thousand students from seventy-nine schools.

STEM

Short for Science, Technology, Engineering, and Math. STEM education has become a priority for business leaders and a growing cadre of American educators.

student assignment plan

A school district's plan for placing children in schools in response to court orders to desegregate. In 2007, the U.S. Supreme Court sharply limited school districts' use of race in such plans. In *Parents Involved in Community Schools v. Seattle School District No. 1 et al.,* the High Court ruled by a 5–4 margin that assignment plans in the Seattle and Jefferson County, Kentucky, districts that classified all students by race, and sometimes relied on race to achieve

Louisville District Unveils New Student-Assignment Plan

By Catherine Gewertz
Education Week: *February 6, 2008*

Seven months after its **student-assignment plan** was struck down by the U.S. Supreme Court, the Jefferson County, Ky., school district has proposed a new system that it hopes will maintain racial, ethnic, and socioeconomic diversity in its schools without running afoul of the law. Jefferson County's new approach bases school assignments on the demographic makeup of the neighborhoods that students live in, rather than on characteristics of individual students.

diversity in individual schools, violated the equal-protection clause of the 14th Amendment.

student identification program

Development of a student identification program is a way for districts or states to keep track of students. By assigning each student a unique identification number, a district can track students when they move between schools and quickly access their records.

student mobility

Student mobility refers to the phenomenon of students changing schools for reasons other than grade promotion. Schools with high rates of student mobility—also referred to as student turnover—generally have one or more of the following characteristics: a large population of children of migrant workers, a large population of homeless children, or a large population of low-income families.

Success for All schools

The Baltimore-based program was founded in 1987 by husband-and-wife researchers Robert E. Slavin and Nancy A. Madden, both of Johns Hopkins University in Baltimore. Success for All is a school reform strategy that operates on the core principles that all children can learn, though not necessarily in exactly the same ways; family and community involvement are crucial; and research offers important guidance on what works in teaching and learning.

summative assessment

Assessment of student learning that seeks to sum up how far students have gotten toward mastery and how well learning aims have been met.

supplemental educational services (SES)

Under the No Child Left Behind Act, schools that fail to make adequate yearly progress for three consecutive years must offer supplemental educational services—free tutoring—to low-income students in the school. Districts must reserve 20 percent of their grants under the federal Title I program to pay for SES. Tutoring under the program is provided by companies, nonprofit groups, and school districts that have received approval from the state.

sustainable school design

Using natural resources and maintenance-free materials in building schools in order to cut energy costs and limit a facility's environmental impact.

takeover

A close cousin to *reconstitution*—the terms are often used interchangeably—a takeover is when a state officially assumes governance of a low-performing school or, much more commonly, an entire district, supplanting the local school board and top school administrators. Takeovers are often a last-resort punishment within state accountability systems, reserved for those beset by mismanagement, infrastructure problems, and declines in student performance.

Takeovers can take a variety of forms. Though they are generally authorized at the state level, the day-to-day control of the affected schools may be assigned to other entities. That approach is behind the growing trend of mayoral takeovers, wherein big-city mayors assume administrative authority over beleaguered urban school systems. Mayoral takeovers have taken place in Boston, Chicago, Cleveland, Detroit, the District of Columbia, New York City, and Oakland (California), among other districts. In a number of cases, takeovers have also dovetailed with appeals for school privatization, with operational control of underperforming schools farmed out to outside school-management firms. (See also *reconstitution*.)

Talent Development model

This school improvement model clusters ninth graders into a separate "Success Academy," usually located on its own floor or wing. Within the academy, students take classes in small learning communities of up to 125 students that share the same teachers. Students also take extended eighty- to ninety-minute block classes and "double doses" of courses in mathematics and language arts and reading. Students spend their remaining high school years in small career academies, where they take courses integrating academic content with their career interests. The Talent Development model was pioneered at Baltimore's Patterson High School in 1994 by researchers from Johns Hopkins University.

teacher certification
A process through which teachers become recognized by the state as expert teachers, implying that they have mastered the complex art of teaching. This is distinguished from a "licensed" teacher, one who practices teaching but is not considered an expert.

teacher licensure
The process by which teachers receive state permission to teach. States typically have minimum requirements such as the completion of certain coursework and experience as a student teacher. Some states, faced with shortages of teachers in particular areas, grant emergency licenses and allow people to take required courses while they are teaching full time.

Teach For America
Teach For America is a national corps of recent college graduates, from all academic majors, who commit two years to teach in urban and rural public schools. The concept was developed by Wendy Kopp during her senior year at Princeton University and was initiated in 1990.

telescoping
Practice of moving a student through instruction in less time than is normal (for example, completing a one-year course in one semester, or three years of middle school in two). Unlike curriculum compacting, telescoping always results in a student advancing to a higher grade level.

Tennessee Value-Added Assessment System (TVAAS)
Enacted in the early 1990s, this system measures the growth students make from the beginning to the end of the school year, based on standardized tests. Teachers and schools are rated on whether their students make more or less progress than a typical student is expected to

make in a given subject and grade, after adjusting for the prior achievement of each child. TVAAS was developed by William L. Sanders and is widely credited with helping to launch nationwide interest in value-added approaches for measuring students' academic progress.

tenure
Tenure offers some job security to teachers who have successfully completed a probationary period on the job. The main reason for tenure is to prevent competent teachers from being fired for arbitrary reasons. Different states and school districts offer different forms of teacher tenure. Tenure at the K–12 level offers less job security than its counterpart in higher education.

test prep
Common shorthand for practices involving preparing students for tests. Test preparation programs have come under fire from critics who complain that teachers spend too much time prepping students for high-stakes standardized tests and not enough time giving children a well-rounded understanding of important topics.

"thin client" computing
One of an emerging array of choices for low-cost computing in schools, "thin client" technology is an arrangement in which many low-capacity computers—or "thin clients"—depend on a powerful central computer server to do most of their data processing. The data is passed back and forth between clients and servers over a network. By contrast, in a "thick client" setup—by far the most common in schools—separate computers perform nearly all their own data processing and use the servers only for communications and data storage.

TIMSS
The Trends in International Mathematics and Science Study, better known as TIMSS, is an international assessment designed to gauge how high school students measure up in math and science comprehension. TIMSS has come to be seen as an important indicator of school achievement and a lever for pushing further reforms in U.S. schools.

Tinker v. *Des Moines Independent School District*
In this 1969 decision, the U.S. Supreme Court held that school officials could not prohibit the expression of student opinion without evidence that the expression would interfere with school discipline or the rights of others. The court said Des Moines school officials could not order

students to remove black armbands they were wearing in school to protest the Vietnam War. The ruling underscored the free speech rights of students in cases where the speech did not disrupt the school environment. (See also *Hazelwood School District* v. *Kuhlmeier.*)

Title I

The federal government's flagship aid program for disadvantaged students, Title I is the largest federal education program for elementary and secondary schools. The program has existed since the Elementary and Secondary Education Act of 1965, when the government first began to authorize formula grants to states and districts for education, and is now encompassed by the No Child Left Behind Act of 2001. Funds under Title I are targeted to high-poverty schools and districts and used to provide educational services to students who are educationally disadvantaged or at risk of failing to meet state standards. With its billions in funding, Title I is the federal government's primary instrument for holding states, districts, and schools accountable for implementing standards-based education. (See also *No Child Left Behind Act.*)

Title IX

The law that bars gender discrimination in education facilities that receive federal funds. The full name of the law is Title IX of the Education Amendments of 1972. The U.S. Supreme Court has ruled that schools may be held liable for sexual harassment of students by their peers or school employees under Title IX. Plaintiffs have also sued schools under Title IX seeking gender equity in extracurricular sports. Separately, the U.S. Department of Education has said that Title IX does not bar schools receiving federal funding from offering single-gender education. (See *sexual harassment* and *single-gender or single-sex education.*)

Title VII of the Elementary and Secondary Education Act

A federal program, created in 1984, to make limited-English-proficient students proficient in the English language. Funding goes to alternative approaches to bilingual education, such as English immersion programs, as well as to traditional instruction in a student's native language. (See *bilingual education* and *limited-English-proficient.*)

Title VII of the of the Civil Rights Act of 1964

Federal law that bars job discrimination based on race, color, religion, sex, and national origin. As employers, schools and school districts must adhere to Title VII or face potential lawsuits if workers charge that they have been the subject of job discrimination.

Total Quality Management

A school-management concept adopted from the business world with a strong focus on client satisfaction and decision-making techniques that encourage workers to seek continual improvement in the organization.

tracking

Tracking is the most commonly used term for ability grouping, the practice of lumping children together according to their academic talents in the classroom. On the elementary level, the divisions sound harmless enough: Kids are divided into the Bluebirds and Redbirds. But in the secondary schools, the stratification becomes more obvious—some say insidious—as students assume their places in the tracking system. (See also *ability grouping, gifted students,* and *special education.*)

transitional bilingual education

A process for educating English-language learners in which instruction for some subjects is in the students' native language, but a certain amount of each day is spent on developing English skills. Classes are made up of students who share the same native language.

transition services

The process by which parents, administrators, and teachers plan for the transition of a child with disabilities from school to life after school. The Individuals with Disabilities Education Act requires that the process be "designed to facilitate the child's movement from school to post-school activities." Transition planning must begin by age sixteen, though some states have lower age requirements. (See also *Individuals with Disabilities Education Act.*)

tribal schools

Schools run by the U.S. Department of the Interior's Bureau of Indian Affairs for Native American children. Most Native American children attend nontribal public schools.

TRIO programs

Federal grants designed to help prepare disadvantaged students for higher education. TRIO traces its roots to three key federal programs launched in the 1960s: Upward Bound, which was launched as part of the Johnson administration's War on Poverty; Talent Search, an outreach program created as part of the Higher Education Act; and Student Support Services, originally known as Special Services for Disadvantaged Students. The term TRIO was coined to describe the original three-pronged program, which later expanded to include other initiatives for needy students.

Troops to Teachers
A program that provides stipends and educational support to military personnel who choose to become teachers in priority subjects and high-need districts. The program is run by the U.S. Department of Education.

truant
A student who is absent from school without permission.

tuition tax credit
State programs that allow parents to receive a tax credit for their children's education expense. Tuition tax credits are a less controversial tool than vouchers for promoting private school choice. (See *school choice* and *vouchers*.)

turnaround specialist
Given that thousands of schools have failed to make adequate progress under the requirements of the federal No Child Left Behind Act, states and districts are looking to "turnaround specialists" to stabilize and rapidly improve poor schools. The idea is borrowed from the private sector. In this case, turnaround specialists are top-notch principals who understand instruction and know how to work with demoralized faculty members.

Turning Points
Based at the Center for Collaborative Learning in Boston, Turning Points is a middle school reform model developed in 1999. It grew out of a landmark national report of the same name that was published by the Carnegie Council on Adolescent Development. Turning Points revolves around seven principles, including teaching a curriculum grounded in standards, involving parents and communities, and governing democratically by all staff members.

twice exceptional (2-E)
A term to describe gifted children with special needs; for example, intellectually gifted children with learning disabilities.

two-way bilingual education

A practice in which instruction is given in two languages to students, usually in the same classroom, who may be dominant in one language or the other, with the goal of the students' becoming proficient in both languages. Teachers usually team teach, with each one responsible to teach in only one of the languages. This approach is also sometimes called *dual-immersion* or *dual-language*.

21st Century Community Learning Centers

Federally supported after-school program. Under the program, states receive funds through formula grants, which they then allocate to school districts, nonprofit organizations, and other recipients to finance after-school and summer programs, particularly for students attending high-poverty schools.

U

universal design for learning (UDL)

The philosophy that advocates creating lessons and classroom materials that are flexible enough to accommodate students' different learning styles.

universal preschool

Government-supported preschool for all young children, not just those identified as at risk for behavioral or learning problems. In an effort to maximize educational gains, educators and policymakers are placing more importance on the education of children in the United States under the age of five. Researchers have found that children exposed to high-quality early education were less likely to drop out of school, repeat grades, or need special education, compared with similar children who did not have such exposure.

Unz initiatives

Nickname for voter initiatives in three states that replaced bilingual education with structured English immersion as the default method for teaching English-language learners. The successful campaigns to pass the initiatives—in California, Arizona, and Massachusetts—were financed by Ron Unz, a Silicon Valley businessman. (See *structured English immersion*.)

V

value-added

A statistical method for determining the impact of a teacher or a school—as compared with other factors such as income level, prior achievement, and school characteristics—on student achievement. Value-added modeling (VAM) or analysis estimates the academic growth a student is expected to make for the year and compares it to how the student actually performs on standardized assessments.

virtual learning environment (VLE)

A computer program designed to facilitate e-learning.

virtual schools

Online schools. With K–12 participation in online learning rapidly expanding, the Southern Regional Education Board (SREB) in 2006 outlined a set of standards for online teaching and offered guidelines on the costs of establishing state virtual schools. SREB's online-teaching report set out eleven standards that teachers should meet, in areas ranging from academic preparation to leadership and management. Online teachers should not only have knowledge of the subjects they teach but also possess technical skills, excellent writing and listening skills, and the ability to handle multiple tasks simultaneously, such as discussion boards, chat tools, and online-instruction groups, SREB said.

The group offered estimates of the cost of running such schools that ranged from $1.5 million to $6 million a year.

vocational education

Instruction that prepares a student for employment immediately after the completion of high school. Although often thought of in terms of auto-shop or carpentry courses, such programs frequently also include a strong academic component and teach cutting-edge skills such as computer-aided design. Today, many proponents refer to "career and technical education" rather than the older term, vocational education. (See also *career and technical education*.)

voucher

A document or chit, usually issued by the state, that can be used by parents to pay tuition at an out-of-district public school, a private school, or a religious school.

Vouchers have been the target of intense criticism as opponents contend they drain away funding from public schools. And, in the case of supplementing religious school tuition, many argue they violate the constitutional principle of separation of church and state. But proponents say vouchers are the only means for some children from lower-income families to obtain an adequate education. And the U.S. Supreme Court rejected church-state separation concerns in the landmark case *Zelman* v. *Simmons-Harris* in 2002. In that ruling, the Court upheld the inclusion of religious schools in a private school voucher program in Cleveland. Church-state issues remain unsettled under many state constitutions. (See also *Zelman* v. *Simmons-Harris*.)

(Lev) Vygotsky

A developmental psychologist, Lev Vygotsky (1896–1934) closely studied the way children learn. He theorized that children had a "zone of proximal development," or an area of learning in which they needed outside assistance to progress. More specifically, he said that, in learning new skills, there are certain tasks that a child cannot perform alone or with similarly skilled peers, but can master only with the help of a more skilled individual. (See *zone of proximal development*.)

Waldorf schools

Private schools based on theories of human development and with a strong emphasis on arts education. The Waldorf education concept was developed by Rudolf Steiner in 1919.

> Vague and the general phrases—"the harmonious development of all the powers and talents in the child," and so forth—cannot provide a basis for a genuine art of education. Such an art of education can only be built on a real knowledge of the human being.
>
> *Rudolf Steiner*. The Education of the Child in the Light of Anthroposophy. *London: Rudolf Steiner Press, 1965*

Web 2.0

A term coined to reflect the new generation of Internet use, which regards the Internet as a platform for information-sharing and community-building rather than an end unto itself.

Wechsler Intelligence Scale for Children (WISC)

An intelligence test for children age six through sixteen that does not require reading or writing. The test is made up of ten core subtests, as well as supplemental assessments. The end result is a full scale score

(FSIQ) and four composite scores for verbal comprehension (VCI), perceptual reasoning (PRI), processing speed (PSI), and working memory (WMI). Another way of putting it is that WISC yields a verbal IQ (VIQ) and performance IQ (PIQ) for those tested, as well as an overall intelligence IQ. The WISC is often used to diagnose attention deficit/hyperactivity disorder and learning disabilities; it is also used in evaluations of potentially gifted children. Large differences in PIQ and VIQ may be indicators of certain types of brain damage. In addition to the WISC, there is a Wechsler Adult Intelligence Scale (WAIS) and a Wechsler Preschool and Primary Scale of Intelligence (WPPSI).

"Weighted" Funding of Schools Gains Favor

By Jeff Archer
Education Week: *November 3, 2004*

Van Asselt Elementary School sits near the southern edge of Seattle in one of the city's most impoverished and ethnically diverse neighborhoods. But on many counts, the school itself is anything but poor when compared with the rest of the district. Tipping the scales in Van Asselt's favor is a budget strategy called **"weighted student" funding.** Rather than allocate staff members to schools on the basis of student enrollment, a weighted-student model divvies up money based on the actual number and kinds of students at each school. Interest in weighted-student funding, which Seattle adopted in 1997, is on the rise among education leaders. San Francisco started using it in 2002. Hawaii, with a single, statewide school system, is in the midst of implementing it. Officials in California and Colorado are studying how they could push the model throughout their states. Not everyone is rushing to adopt weighted-student funding, which is linked closely to site-based management. Proponents of centralized management say there are other ways to reduce inequities without shifting considerable decisionmaking authority over financial matters to schools, as almost all of the districts that use weighted-student funding have done.

weighted-student funding

A weighted-student model allocates school funding not just on the basis of how many students attend a school but on the educational needs of those students. This means that schools whose students have greater needs (for example, poor, disabled, or English-language-learner pupils) would receive more funding than those with the same number of students but fewer at-risk learners. Weighted-student funding is linked closely to site-based management. By contrast, most districts use a more traditional staff-based budgeting system—for example, one in which a school might hire another teacher or other staffer for every twenty-five students.

What Works Clearinghouse

An online clearinghouse supported by the U.S. Department of Education that vets the evidence base for educational programs, practices, and policies.

whole-school change

A strategy of implementing schoolwide change in struggling schools. In 1991, business leaders created a nonprofit organization that underwrote the New American Schools project, which was tasked with drawing up comprehensive plans for turning around failing schools. Today, nonprofit and for-profit companies pursue whole-school reform methods, frequently in inner-city districts. (See *Comer schools, EdisonLearning, KIPP schools,* and *Success for All.*)

whole language

A philosophy and instructional strategy that emphasizes reading for meaning and in context. Although teachers may give phonics lessons to individual students as needed, the emphasis is on teaching students to consider words and text as a whole rather than focusing on individual segments within a word. (See also *phonics.*)

wiki

A wiki is an Internet site that allows anyone with access to it the ability to add or edit the content on the site. Wikis were originally used by software engineers to collaborate on writing software and for other technical tasks. Wikis have caught on among some teachers, who have developed creative ways of using them in their classrooms. Some school administrators are also turning to wikis to help them do their jobs. Wiki is an abbreviated version of *wiki-wiki,* a Hawaiian word that translates as "quick" in English. Wikipedia.org is probably the world's most famous wiki.

year-round education

A modified school calendar that offers short breaks throughout the academic year rather than the traditional summer vacation. Schools may use a year-round schedule for a variety of reasons, including staggering schedules to relieve crowding. Others believe that shorter gaps between periods of schooling will help students retain material.

youth apprenticeship

Student preparation for an entry-level job through a combination of workplace learning and academic work. Apprenticeships can either be paid or unpaid. (See *career and technical education* and *vocational education*.)

Zelman v. *Simmons-Harris*

A 2002 U.S. Supreme Court decision holding that an Ohio law allowing religious schools to participate in a private school voucher program for low-income families in Cleveland did not violate the First Amendment's prohibition against government establishment of religion. Because parents made the decision where to direct state voucher aid, the program was one of "true private choice" and thus was neutral toward religion, the court majority said.

zero-tolerance policies

Practices in place in some schools and districts that exact strict discipline in cases where students bring weapons—or drugs—to school. Under a strictly enforced zero-tolerance policy, a student found with any weapon on school property would be immediately suspended or expelled.

zone of proximal development

A term coined by Russian developmental psychologist Lev Vygotsky. It refers to activities a child cannot perform alone or with others of the same ability, but can perform with help from other, more skilled individuals. (See *(Lev) Vygotsky.*)

Organizations and Other Terms

A Guide to Acronyms and Other Challenging Language

Note: In cases where an organization's name does not clearly explain what the organization does or whom it represents, a brief description is provided.

Education Organizations

(The) Arc: Formerly, the Association for Retarded Citizens of the United States.

(U.S.) DOE: Department of Education.

AACTE: American Association of Colleges for Teacher Education.

AASA: American Association of School Administrators.

AASL: American Association of School Librarians, a division of the American Library Association (ALA).

AASPA: American Association of School Personnel Administrators.

ABCTE: American Board for the Certification of Teacher Excellence.

ACE: American Council on Education. ACE is a Washington-based umbrella group for higher education.

ACT: The nonprofit testing organization that produces the ACT college-entrance exam. ACT was founded in 1959 as the American College Testing program.

ACTFL: American Council on the Teaching of Foreign Languages.

AERA: American Educational Research Association.

AFT: American Federation of Teachers. The nation's second-largest teachers' union.

AIR: American Institutes for Research.

ASBO: Association of School Business Officials International.

ASCA: American School Counselors Association.

ASCD: Association for Supervision and Curriculum Development.

ATE: Association of Teacher Educators.

CAL: Center for Applied Linguistics. CAL promotes and seeks to improve the teaching and learning of languages.

CALDER: National Center for the Analysis of Longitudinal Data in Education Research.

CASEL: Collaborative for Academic, Social, and Emotional Learning.

CASTLE: Center for Advanced Study of Technology Leadership in Education.

CCSSO: Council of Chief State School Officers.

CEC: Council for Exceptional Children. CEC is dedicated to improving education for children with disabilities and exceptionalities, as well as students identified as gifted.

Center for CSRI: Center for Comprehensive School Reform and Improvement.

CES: Coalition of Essential Schools. A nonprofit network of schools, centers, groups, and individuals seeking to create personalized, intellectually challenging schools.

CGCS: Council of the Great City Schools. CGCS is a national advocacy organization representing the nation's urban school systems.

CIERA: Center for the Improvement of Early Reading Achievement.

CLE: Center for Law and Education. CLE assists low-income students and low-income communities in addressing public education problems.

CoSN: Consortium for School Networking. The Washington-based CoSN is an advocacy group for educational technology.

Council for Opportunity in Education: A Washington-based organization that advocates for TRIO programs, which are federally supported higher education initiatives.

CPRE: Consortium for Policy Research in Education.

CRESST: Center for Research on Evaluation, Standards, and Student Testing.

CTQ: Center for Teacher Quality.

Data Quality Campaign. A coalition of education groups led by the National Center on Educational Accountability.

ECS: Education Commission of the States.

ERIC: Education Resource Information Center.

ETS: Educational Testing Service. ETS is the nonprofit corporation that produces the SAT college-entrance exam and the Praxis teacher-certification exams.

FairTest: The National Center for Fair and Open Testing.

HELP Committee: The U.S. Senate's Health, Education, Labor, and Pensions Committee.

IATEFL: International Association of Teachers of English as a Foreign Language.

ICLE: International Center for Leadership in Education.

IEA: International Association for the Evaluation of Educational Achievement.

IES: Institute of Education Sciences.

INCA: International Review of Curriculum and Assessment Frameworks.

IRA: International Reading Association.

ISKME: Institute for the Study of Knowledge Management in Education.

ISLLC: Interstate School Leaders Licensure Consortium.

ISTE: International Society for Technology in Education.

ITEA: International Technology Education Association.

KIPP: Knowledge Is Power Program. KIPP is a network of charter schools.

LDA: Learning Disabilities Association of America.

LULAC: League of United Latin American Citizens.

McREL: Mid-Continent Research for Education and Learning.

MENC: The National Association for Music Education. This organization was formerly called the Music Educators National Conference, and it retains its original initials.

MLA: Modern Language Association.

NAACP: National Association for the Advancement of Colored People.

NAACP Legal Defense Fund. The organization pursues legal action in school desegregation.

NACAC: National Association for College Admission Counseling.

NACOL: North American Council for Online Learning.

NAESP: National Association of Elementary School Principals.

NAEYC: National Association for the Education of Young Children.

NAFIS: National Association of Federally Impacted Schools.

NAGB: National Assessment Governing Board.

NAGC: National Association for Gifted Children.

NAPCS: National Alliance for Public Charter Schools.

NASBE: National Association of State Boards of Education.

NASDSE: National Association of State Directors of Special Education.

NASDTEC: National Association of State Directors of Teacher Education and Certification.

NASPE: National Association for Sport and Physical Education.

NASS: National Association of Street Schools.

NASSP: National Association of Secondary School Principals.

NBPTS: National Board for Professional Teaching Standards.

NCATE: National Council for Accreditation of Teacher Education.

NCCEP: National Council for Community and Education Partnerships.

NCEA: National Center on Educational Accountability. An Austin, Texas-based nonprofit group that supports data-based efforts to improve schools.

NCEE: National Center on Education and the Economy.

NCEE: National Council on Economic Education.

NCER: National Center for Education Research.

NCES: National Center for Education Statistics.

NCHE: National Council for History Education.

NCIEA: National Center for the Improvement of Educational Assessment.

NCPIE: National Coalition for Parent Involvement in Education.

NCRECE: National Center for Research on Early Childhood Education.

NCREL: North Central Regional Educational Laboratory.

NCSS: National Council for the Social Studies.

NCTAF: National Council on Teaching and America's Future.

NCTE: National Council of Teachers of English.

NCTL: National Center for Technological Literacy.

NCTM: National Council of Teachers of Mathematics.

NCTQ: National Council on Teacher Quality.

NEA: National Education Association. NEA is the nation's largest teachers' union, with 3.2 million members in 2008.

NEA: National Endowment for the Arts.

NECC: National Educational Computing Conference.

NEH: National Endowment for the Humanities.

NGA: National Governors Association.

NICHCY: National Dissemination Center for Children with Disabilities. This organization was formerly called the National Information Center for Children and Youth with Disabilities, and it retains its original initials.

NICHD: National Institute of Child Health and Human Development.

NIEA: National Indian Education Association.

NIL: National Institute for Literacy.

NILD: National Institute for Learning Development.

NLNS: New Leaders for New Schools.

NMSA: National Middle School Association.

NRC/GT: National Research Center on the Gifted and Talented.

NRC: National Research Council.

NSBA: National School Boards Association.

NSDC: National Staff Development Council.

NSF: National Science Foundation.

NSTA: National Science Teachers Association.

NUA: National Urban Alliance.

OCR: Office for Civil Rights. OCR is the office within the U.S. Department of Education tasked with investigating complaints of discrimination within schools.

OCRE: Organizations Concerned About Rural Education.

OECD: Organization for Economic Cooperation and Development, based in Paris

OSEP: Office of Special Education Programs.

OSERS: Office of Special Education and Rehabilitative Services.

PACE: Policy Analysis for California Education. PACE is a nonprofit research group based at the University of California, Berkeley.

Partnership for 21st Century Skills: This is a Tucson, Arizona-based coalition of business and education groups that advocates infusing skills into education that are needed in the workplace.

PEN: Public Education Network.

Pre-K Now: A Washington-based advocacy group

PTA: Parent Teacher Association. The national organization describes itself as "the largest volunteer child advocacy association" in the United States.

PTO: Parent-teacher organization. PTOs are school-based groups unaffiliated with the National PTA. Some PTOs call themselves HSAs (Home and School Associations) or PCCs (Parent Communication Councils).

SAIS: Southern Association of Independent Schools.

SREB: Southern Regional Education Board.

TESOL: Teachers of English to Speakers of Other Languages.

TFA: Teach For America.

TLN: Teacher Leaders Network.

TNTP: The New Teacher Project.

USDLA: United States Distance Learning Association. The USDLA is a Boston-based nonprofit organization with 4,500 members nationwide that promotes the development and application of distance learning for education and training.

WestEd: WestEd is a nonprofit research, development, and service agency with expertise in testing and accountability, early-childhood and youth development, and program evaluation, among other areas.

WIDA: World-Class Instructional Design and Assessment. WIDA is a consortium made up of eighteen states working to improve conditions for English-language learners.

WWC: What Works Clearinghouse. Established by the U.S. Department of Education in 2002, WWC defines itself as "a central and trusted source of scientific evidence for what works in education."

ZERO TO THREE: National Center for Infants, Toddlers and Families.

Key Laws and Terms

AAC: augmentative and alternative communication.

ADA: Americans with Disabilities Act.

AD/HD: attention deficit/hyperactivity disorder (ADD refers to attention deficit disorder).

AMO: annual measurable objective.

AP: Advanced Placement.

ASL: American sign language.

AYP: adequate yearly progress.

CAPD: central auditory processing disorder.

CMO: charter management organization.

CMS: course-management system.

DAS: Differential Abilities Scales.

DI: direct instruction.

DIBELS: Dynamic Indicators of Basic Early Literacy Skills.

ELL: English-language learner.

EMO: education management organization.

ESEA: Elementary and Secondary Education Act.

ESL: English as a second language.

FAFSA: Free Application for Federal Student Aid.

FAPE: free, appropriate public education.

FERPA: Family Educational Rights and Privacy Act.

GED: General Educational Development. A credential that can be earned in place of a high school diploma for those individuals who drop out of school or cannot finish their diploma work otherwise.

GPA: grade point average.

GT: gifted and talented.

HBCU: historically black college or university.

HEA: Higher Education Act.

HOTS: higher-order thinking skills.

HOUSSE: High Objective Uniform State Standard of Evaluation. HOUSSE is a provision of the No Child Left Behind Act.

IB: International Baccalaureate.

IBB: interest-based bargaining.

IDEA: Individuals with Disabilities Education Act.

IEP: individualized education program.

IQ: intelligence quotient.

KERA: Kentucky Education Reform Act.

LCES: low socioeconomic status.

LEA: local education agency (a school district, in other words).

LEF: local education fund.

LEP: limited-English-proficient.

LD: learning disability or learning disabled.

LMS: learning management system.

LRE: least restrictive environment.

NAEP: National Assessment of Educational Progress.

NBCT: national board certified teacher.

NCLB: No Child Left Behind Act.

NETS-T: National Educational Technology Standards for Teachers.

NLD: nonverbal learning disorder.

OBE: outcomes-based education.

ODD: oppositional defiant disorder.

OER: open educational resources.

PALS: phonological awareness literacy screening.

PDD-NOS: pervasive developmental disorder-not otherwise specified.

PDK: Phi Delta Kappa.

PIRC: parent information and resource center.

PIRLS: Progress in International Reading Literacy Study.

PISA: Program for International Student Assessment.

PIQ: Performance IQ.

PLC: professional learning community.

RSD: Recovery School District (the New Orleans school system after Hurricane Katrina).

RTI: response to intervention.

SASS: Schools and Staffing Survey.

SAT: Formerly the Scholastic Aptitude Test.

SBE: scientifically based evidence.

SBR: scientifically based research.

SEA: state education agency.

SEL: social and emotional learning.

SES: supplemental educational services or socioeconomic status.

SID: sensory integration disorder.

SIF: School Interoperability Framework.

SIOP: sheltered instruction observation protocol.

STEM: science, technology, engineering, and math.

TIMSS: Third International Mathematics and Science Study.

VIQ: Verbal IQ.

VLE: virtual learning environment.

WISC: Wechsler Intelligence Scale for Children.

Grateful acknowledgment is made for permission to print the following:

"'Book Study' Helps Teachers Hone Skills," by Bess Keller, as first appeared in *Education Week*, May 21, 2008. Reprinted with permission from Editorial Projects in Education.

"Managers Team Up to Run Charters," by Caroline Hendrie, as first appeared in *Education Week*, June 15, 2005. Reprinted with permission from Editorial Projects in Education.

"Market for K-12 Course-Management Systems Expands," by Andrew Trotter, as first appeared in *Education Week*, February 27, 2008. Reprinted with permission from Editorial Projects in Education.

"Instructional Model May Yield Gains for English-Learners," by Mary Ann Zehr, as first appeared in *Education Week*, December 5, 2007. Reprinted with permission from Editorial Projects in Education.

"U.S. Judge Rules Intelligent Design Has No Place in Science Classrooms," by Sean Cavanagh, as first appeared in *Education Week*, December 20, 2005. Reprinted with permission from Editorial Projects in Education.

"With World Growing Smaller, IB Gets Big," by Scott J. Cech, as first appeared in *Education Week*, October 31, 2007. Reprinted with permission from Editorial Projects in Education.

"'Looping' Catches On as a Way to Build Strong Ties," by Linda Jacobson, as first appeared in *Education Week*, October 15, 1997. Reprinted with permission from Editorial Projects in Education.

"Teacher Re-Creation," by Jeff Archer, as first appeared in *Education Week*, January 10, 2001. Reprinted with permission from Editorial Projects in Education.

"Software Solution Saves Dollars," by Andrew Trotter, as first appeared in *Education Week*, September 29, 2004. Reprinted with permission from Editorial Projects in Education.

"States Giving Performance Pay by Doling Out Bonuses," by Michele McNeil, as first appeared in *Education Week*, September 6, 2006. Reprinted with permission from Editorial Projects in Education.

"Working Smarter By Working Together," by Vaishali Honawar, as first appeared in *Education Week*, April 2, 2008. Reprinted with permission from Editorial Projects in Education.

"'Response to Intervention' Sparks Interest, Questions," by Christina A. Samuels, as first appeared in *Education Week*, January 23, 2008. Reprinted with permission from Editorial Projects in Education.

Sample SAT-style questions from *SAT For Dummies*® 2005, 6th ed. by Geraldine Woods. Reprinted with permission from publisher.

"Md. Service Learning: Classroom Link Weak?," by Michelle Galley, as first appeared in *Education Week*, October 15, 2003. Reprinted with permission from Editorial Projects in Education.

"Louisville District Unveils New Students-Assignment Plan," by Catherine Gewertz, as first appeared in *Education Week*, February 6, 2008. Reprinted with permission from Editorial Projects in Education.

"'Weighted' Funding of Schools Gains Favor," by Jeff Archer, as first appeared in *Education Week*, November 3, 2004. Reprinted with permission from Editorial Projects in Education.